BURIED & SUNKEN TREASURE

A Golden Hands book

Marshall Cavendish, London

Acknowledgements
John Condon and John Whittle
of the Old Bottle Cellar

Picture Sources
Aerofilms 100-101; Chris Barker 112-113; British
Museum 80, 83, 86, 92, 93; Courtesy of British Museum
36, 41, 42-43, 81, 84-85, 87; British Tourist Authority 91;
Rex Cowan 5, 8-9, 10, 12, 13, 14, 16, 17, 18, 19, 20, 22,
23, 24-25, 27, 28, 29, 32, 33; Daily Telegraph,
London/Photographer Paul Armiger 30-31; Department
of the Environment 96-97; Mary Evans Picture Library
104, 106, 107, 114-115, 119; C.M. Frederick 65, 66-67,
71 (top), 74, 75, 77 (top), 78, 79; Jim Gill 54, 57, 60, 61,
62; Steven Halliday 48, 50; Michael Holford 81, 88-89;
London Illustrated News 34, 35; Mansell Collection 66,
109, 111; Robert Marx 68-69, 71 (bottom), 72, 73, 120;
National Maritime Museum 7; National Monuments
Record/Photographer Colonel G. Meates
99/Photographer Iva Dundas 102; Old Bottle Cellar,
London/Photographer Leo Zanelli 38-39, 44, 45, 46-47;
Picturepoint 94-95; Sjohistoriska Museum, Sweden 77
(bottom); Spectrum 82; The Times, London 40; Tri-Art
51, 53, 56, 58-59.

Edited by Windsor Chorlton

Published by Marshall Cavendish Publications Limited,
58 Old Compton Street,
London WIV 5PA

© Marshall Cavendish Publications Limited 1974

This volume first published 1974

Printed by Henri Proost, Turnhout, Belgium

ISBN 0 85685 063 2

This volume is not to be sold in
the USA, Canada or the Philippines

ABOUT THIS BOOK

Few things capture the imagination more than stories of treasure and treasure hunting. But how true are the mysterious tales of gold-laden galleons; and what are the chances of finding some long-lost hoard which will make you rich for life?

This book takes a factual, exciting and up-to-date look at a subject which is more popular than ever before, and which has become big business during the last few years. As well as describing the amazing finds made in recent years, it reveals some of the revolutionary techniques employed by the professional treasure hunters.

Among the true-life treasure quests recounted here is the saga of the *Liefde* – a richly-laden East Indiaman discovered in the Shetlands 250 years after she sank. Another chapter details the headline-hitting story of the wrecks salvaged in the Scillies – the *Association*, plundered by 20th century pirates after she had been located by Navy divers; the *Hollandia*, tracked down after months of careful research. And, of course, there are pages devoted to the recent recoveries in the Caribbean – graveyard of the Spanish Plate Fleets.

Nearer home, a well-known treasure hunter tells of the riches discovered by accident in Britain; and reveals that the possibility of discovering gold beneath your feet is greater than you might think. And for the would-be treasure hunter there is a discussion of the law of Treasure Trove and the controversial use of metal detectors.

Although *Buried and Sunken Treasure* concentrates on real treasures and treasure hunts, no book on this subject would be complete without mention of some legendary pirate hoard which has eluded searchers for centuries. The backgrounds to two of these hoards – reputed to have been buried by Captain Kidd and Henry Morgan – make a fascinating end-piece.

Buried and Sunken Treasure is a must for the armchair-adventurer who likes an authentically exciting tale well-told. Written by experts and illustrated with many unique photographs which capture the excitement of treasure hunting, it cannot fail to strike a responsive chord in any reader who has ever dreamed of discovering a treasure hoard.

CONTENTS

WRECKS ROUND THE SCILLIES

Richard Larn

To the majority of people, sunken treasure is automatically associated with the Spanish Main; with pirates, galleons, and tropical islands, whereas in fact there is as much gold and silver on the sea-bed around the British Isles as anywhere else in the world. It is also a fallacy that successful treasure hunting underwater is the prerogative of a select and privileged few. Anyone with a small capital outlay, determination, and single mindedness can experience for

Above. *Gold coins and a ring recovered from the Association. The discovery of this ship sparked off a new interest in treasure hunting.*

himself the thrill of finding long sunken coins, or other valuables.

Treasure, which can take many forms, has a strange attraction for men, which extends beyond the old adage of 'something for nothing', and often beyond the actual value of the items sought. For as long as men have been capable of working underwater, there have been individuals prepared to risk their fortune, even their lives, to this end. Most books concerning diving history would have us believe that prolonged and successful salvage, at even relatively modest depths, was not possible until the late 18th century, which proves how little they researched the subject.

Obviously they had not heard of such men as Jacob Johnson, Captain Rowe, Archibald Miller, John Lethbridge and others. Between the years of 1620 and 1760, this select band of adventurers worked on any wreck of value between the Shetland Isles and South Africa, recovering impressive quantities of gold and silver, jewels, bronze cannon and other valuables. Jacob Johnson, or to give him his commonly accepted title, 'Jacob the diver', was so successful in his occupation that his services were in constant demand by nobility and admiralty alike.

The first treasure hunters

During October 1627, the *Green Dragon* and the *Campen,* two ships belonging to the Dutch East India Company, were wrecked on the Needles, at the south-western point of the Isle of Wight. Van Ommerman, the Deputy of the Company, came to an agreement with 'Jacob the diver' concerning salvage, and by May 1629, some 2360 reales of eight, five bronze cannon, 101 ingots of lead, and nine anchors had been recovered – from an area renowned for its vicious tides and poor underwater visibility. Jacob stated that he regularly worked at a depth of six fathoms and, when necessary, at ten fathoms but that: 'I was exceedingly uncomfortable and my ears bled'.

Of the other early divers, Captain Rowe appears to have favoured the north of England and Scotland, and established his reputation by salvaging specie from the Dutch East Indiaman *Lastdrager* (1653), and other wrecks in the vicinity of the Shetlands – some as far afield as the more remote parts of Ireland.

Archibald Miller concentrated on the west coast mainly and, in particular, worked for the Duke of Argyll, who owned the rights to the Tobermory Bay wreck, which had been an Armada ship. Last but not least was John Lethbridge, a west country man from Newton Abbot, in Devon, who appeared on the scene

long after Johnson and Miller were dead. He enjoyed the advantages of an improved diving apparatus which he designed and built himself, and it was here that his skill and craftsmanship as a cooperer was an advantage, since his 'diving engine' bore a marked resemblance to a barrel. Like Jacob Johnson before him, Lethbridge travelled far and wide to the site of valuable shipwrecks, and as a result became a very accomplished salvage diver. But, as will be seen later, there was at least one wreck over which he had to admit defeat.

The exploits of these pioneers, who generally were more than successful, has not had a marked influence on modern salvage, since they left behind them very little record of their work and hence we have inherited a legacy of uncertainty. There is an understandable, but erroneous tendency amongst treasure hunters and amateur researchers, to assume that, because a particular incident or piece of information is new to them, they have made an original, possibly unique discovery. This could prove to be an expensive mistake if, for example, acting only on a few elementary scraps of information, a costly underwater search was instituted to find a particular wreck site. One should never underestimate the ability or skill of our predecessors: if a particular wreck was known to be carrying anything of value when it was lost, then every effort would be made to effect its recovery. Money was just as important to people three hundred years ago as it is today; so that in the majority of modern salvage attempts on old wrecks, it would be unrealistic to presume that no one had been there before. With early salvage work so successful, current attempts are often confined to merely 'picking up the crumbs', the bulk of any real treasure having been taken long ago.

Treasure island Britain

The British Isles have a total of 67 counties which border the sea, and every one of them can lay claim to at least one treasure wreck. Some counties can justly claim a great many such

Top right. *A 16th century map shows the route of the ill-fated Spanish Armada of 1588.*
Bottom right. *After the crucial battle between the Spanish and English fleets, the beaten Armada tried to run for home. Storms wrecked the fleet off the Irish and Scottish coasts.*

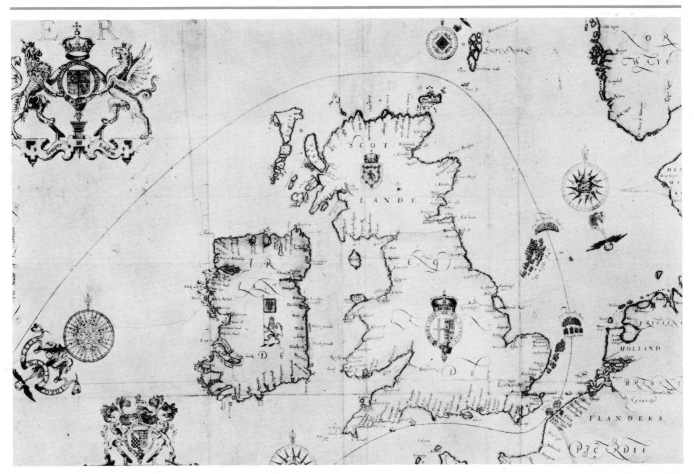

wrecks, in particular those on the west coast of Ireland, since it was here that a score of vessels from the defeated Spanish Armada came to grief.

Another lucrative area is the Shetland Isles, which can claim not only Armada ships, but predominantly vessels of the Dutch East India Company. A great many of these old wrecks have been found over recent years, and the overall value of the recovered material is considerable, but far from consistent in each individual case. When the remains of the Armada ship *Santa Maria de la Rose* were finally located in Blasket Sound, southern Ireland, after many months of searching in 1968, two pewter plates, a medallion, a few silver and one gold coin, were poor reward. In contrast, it cost the people of Ulster approximately £130,000 to purchase the treasure salvaged from the Armada galleass *Girona,* researched and located by Robert Stenuit. This wreck was found near the Giants Causeway, Co Antrim, in 1967, close to an outcrop known as Spaniards Rock! As a result, a spectacular collection of 16th century jewellery, coins and trinkets is now on permanent display in the Belfast Museum. But this is regrettably the only instance in which salvaged material has been retained as a collection, and not put up for public auction.

Recent discoveries in the Shetland Isles include the *Liefde* (1711); the *Lastdrager* (1653); *Kenermerlandt* (1664); *Wendela* (1737); *Curacao* (1729); and the *Evstafii* (1780) – all of which have yielded valuable coins and historic items. But even this impressive list is totally eclipsed by salvage carried out in the Isles of Scilly, Cornwall – an area which, today, has proven to be the most lucrative source of sunken treasure in Britain.

The ship's graveyard

Situated 28 miles from Lands End, the Isles of Scilly consist of a group of some 145 islands and rocks; none of which reach higher than 200 feet above sea level. In winter they are lashed by gale after gale, or else are enshrouded by fog for

Right. *A heavy sea breaks over the reef which claimed the* **Association.** *In the age of sailing ships the rocks and shoals of the Scillies were a death trap. The inset shows the Naval diving team who carried out the recent research which led to the location of the Scillies' wrecks.*

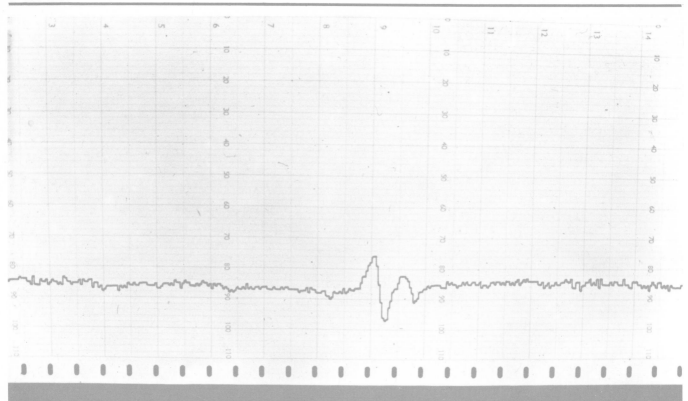

days at a time. It needs but little imagination to realise how remote and isolated the inhabitants must have been 250 years ago or more. As for shipwrecks, there have been so many that no one knows the total, and the wreck list produced by the local museum committee is constantly being amended to include some new name, derived either from the archives, or from the sea itself by divers.

Treasure hunting and marine archaeology in the British Isles are indebted to the Isles of Scilly, since it was here, during the summer of 1964, that a chance underwater find led to the eventual relocation of HMS *Association* three years later. The expression 'relocation' is used in preference to such verbs as 'discovered' or 'found', since as with the majority of wreck sites, it was never really lost, only forgotten. It was not the relocation of the site that was important, but rather what was found on the site that was significant, since from this focal point stemmed the finding of three more treasure ships in the Isles of Scilly, and the majority of those already mentioned in other parts of the country.

Until 1964, no one seriously believed that old wrecks could survive the rigours of British waters; the remains of old ships found to date were always in the calm waters of the Medi-

Above. *No device has helped the treasure hunter more than the magnetometer. A signal from hidden metal is clearly shown on the screen.*

terranean, and a number of self-appointed authorities on the subject even went so far as to express openly that, 'marine archaeology will never be practised in this country'. This assumption was based on the speed with which the sea around the United Kingdom could demolish a modern steel ship, and a marked preference for University sponsored expeditions to take place in the sunlit waters of Greece, rather than in the cold, murky conditions of the Atlantic.

First dives

In 1964, the Naval Air Command Sub Aqua Club (NAC-SAC) had been an officially recognised body within the Royal Navy for only three years. Its first completely seaborne diving expedition was to the Isles of Scilly that year; the objective of the ten divers aboard being to generally search for shipwrecks of any vintage, in particular that of the Genoese barque *Indipendenza,* lost on the Barrel of Butter rock on 24 September 1881. It was hoped that some of the thousands of animal horns she carried as cargo might have survived.

The activities of the divers took them to an offshore rock near Old Town, known as the Gilstone; and it was here that one iron cannon and an old anchor were found in deep water. Discussion with some of the locals in the Mermaid Inn at Hugh Town suggested that they had found the site of the *Association*– completely by accident. Its accessibility to the mainland of St Marys suggested that complete salvage had been carried out, leaving only the two remaining items. Only then, when it was time for the expedition to leave the islands for the mainland, was it learnt that there were, in fact, two rocks named Gilstone, one of which the Navy team had searched, the other, known as the Outer Gilstone, being some seven miles away to the south-west, close to the Bishop rock and its famous lighthouse.

That winter, efforts were made to research into the *Association,* and the story that unfolded had all the elements of a fictional thriller – except that it was mostly true. The story had everything – a great fleet of British warships under a famous admiral, returning home after a successful campaign in the Mediterranean in 1707; great chests of gold and silver coins aboard the flagship, plus what was loosely described as 'the Queen's plate'. There were stories of a lowly seaman warning the great admiral, Sir Cloudesley Shovell, of danger if he continued on his present course, and of the seaman being hung from the yardarm for his impertinence. The stories told of the sinking of the *Association* along with three other ships, and of 2000 men being drowned, the former with no survivors except the admiral himself, who was murdered on the beach for the rings he wore. And woven throughout this fantastic story was the constant reference to treasure; to the ten great chests of gold and silver carried by the *Association.* No mention was made of salvage.

Considerably wiser regarding local geography, and armed with the knowledge that the *Association* had struck and sunk on the Bishop and Clerks rocks – a name that unfortunately is no longer in use, but is presumed to imply the Outer Gilstone area – the Navy team tackled this part of the western rocks in 1965. South-westerly gales and huge seas pounded over the reef for the majority of their stay and, except for a few random dives in the approximate location, very little constructive work was done. One thing, though, that sustained the team was that the research carried out over the winter months, limited though it had been, had not only revealed some information about the *Association,* but also suggested that there had been a number of other valuable ships lost in the Scillies; at least two of which could be classified as treasure ships. But, until one such vessel was found, there was no way of telling what condition they were in, or whether any valuables remained to be salvaged.

Beginning of a legal battle

Legally, of course, the remains of the doomed fleet still belonged to the Royal Navy, so although their action was setting a precedent in the service, the NAC-SAC team made an application to the Admiralty for a contract or licence to search for and, if successful, to salvage the remains of the wrecked ships concerned. Naturally their Lordships were somewhat taken aback: what on earth were serving members of the Navy doing asking for a contract to salvage' vessels which belonged to their own service? Perhaps it was only seen as a publicity stunt for an activity which was considered as somewhat eccentric anyway.

It took a very long time for the application to grind its way from the desk of Flag Officer (Air), at Lee-on-Solent, to Whitehall; from there to the historical branch who checked on the authenticity of the claim; back to Whitehall; and then on to the contracts division of the Navy, situated at Bath. By this time it was 1966, and the Navy divers were back in the Scillies, more determined than ever to find the wreck they sought. Only now, both local and national newspapers had latched onto the treasure aspects of the venture, and lurid headlines announced 'Navy Divers Seek £1million Treasure'; which shortly after, when it wasn't found in the first two or three days, was magnified to a cool £3million!

This unwanted publicity naturally attracted a lot of attention and, prompted by the knowledge that the Navy team had applied for a contract to salvage, two other organisations applied for contracts to salvage the very same ships. In spite of the fact that the Navy team's application had been in official hands for months already, incredible though it may seem, the appropriate department issued, not one contract, but three – and for the same operation! How on earth they

Above. *Bad weather hampered the Naval team in their search for the **Association** and it took three years before divers located the wreck.*
Left. *Among the first objects to be recovered from the site of the **Association** were cannon. The rich finds soon attracted treasure 'pirates'.*

hoped to resolve the situation in the event of the wrecks being found cannot be imagined. It can only be presumed that they were completely out of their depth; were attempting to please everyone; or else presumed that no one was really serious, and that nothing would be found.

The 1966 Naval expedition was also plagued with bad weather, and only one dive was possible in the vicinity of the Outer Gilstone, in a two week period. However, on returning the following year, everything was in their favour. Not only was the weather perfect, with mirror-calm seas and clear skies, but the team now had a trump card. Over the winter of 1966, one of their number had located the original Admiralty

survey chart of the Scillies, prepared by Grahame Spence in 1740. On this hand-drawn chart, the rock known today as the Outer Gilstone was clearly marked Shovel rock. It could not be clearer or more obvious that this was where the admiral and his flagship came to grief.

Why the name of this rock with such an historical connection had been changed, and when this change occurred, is still a mystery. The most likely explanation is that it was changed by the locals after the wreck of the fleet, in order to hide the true location – or was it changed by the authorities? As will be seen later, this is not the only suggestion of a royal cover up over a treasure wreck in the islands.

On 2 July 1967, the Navy team commenced a systematic search of the reef, but nothing was seen that day, nor the next. But then, on 4 July, the team put divers between the Gilstone rock and Gilstone Ledge, on the peak of the reef where the water is shallowest. They landed smack down on a great mass of cannon; the long search for the *Association* was over.

The 'pirates' move in

When faced with the stark reality that the historic wreck they sought was there, right beneath their feet, it was almost an anti-climax. But then the implications of the discovery sank in and it was realised that what was needed now was time. Time to search the entire site and establish what really remained of this 90 gun warship – but most of all, time to think clearly. For most people, the finding of a treasure wreck is a 'once in a lifetime' experience, and it takes a little getting used to the idea.

Unfortunately, time was the one thing the team did not have, and so decisions were rushed. In an attempt to gain more time on the site, they were forced to disclose the fact that the fabled *Association* had been found, and that they had already raised bronze cannon, along

Below. *Rex Cowan (in centre of group), a London solicitor, followed the excavation of the* **Association** *with interest, and was impelled to seek out other ships lost in the Scillies.*

with gold and silver coins. Perhaps in different circumstances, the Ministry of Defence would have had time to withdraw the other two contracts and claim the wreck as their property. Certainly that is what everyone expected them to do, especially since the only diving team to appear on the Gilstone in the past three years had been the Navy team. Instead, the three contracts were left open, the authorities disassociated themselves from the very wreck for which they had previously been issuing contracts, and their publicity department released the news of the find to the newspapers.

The knowledge that gold and silver coins and bronze cannon lay on the sea-bed for the asking amongst the rocks of the Isles of Scilly, was communicated to the world. News of the find appeared in newspapers as far away as Hong Kong and the Pacific. Naturally, this brought to south-west England just about every freelance diver in the business, and a mad scramble began. It was more than degrading for the Navy team to watch their wreck being torn to pieces, and to listen to radio and television reports how this civilian team had found the site 'after years of searching', or how that team had 'fulfilled a boyhood dream'. In fact, six months after the relocation, it was difficult to convince anyone that a Navy team had ever been involved.

Exactly how much treasure was taken from the *Association* will never be known. With the certain knowledge that the Crown would claim at least 50 per cent, if not 75 per cent of anything handed in to the Receiver of Wrecks, in accordance with the law of salvage, there was no incentive for people to be particularly honest. When faced with the decision whether or not to hand in and declare say, twenty gold coins, for which a diver had fought hard, and in some measure risked his life, to eventually receive £500 in return; or keep quiet and pocket their real value of some £2,000, then legality can take on a different aspect.

The rape of the *Association*

It is a requirement of British law that when items are salvaged from the sea and declared, a public notice to this effect must be displayed. This notice remains on view for a year and a day, in order to give the possible rightful owner time to claim his property. The board used for this purpose in the Isles of Scilly is situated on the quay at Hugh Town, St Marys, and

throughout the whole *Association* saga made interesting reading.

But it was obvious from the outset that for every hundred or more silver coins declared by divers, there might be only one gold, or none at all. With as many as five different teams diving on the site at the same time, and a changing population in each team, there is no knowing what was found. Certainly few divers left the Gilstone empty handed. Some divers, either more fortunate or determined than others, had days when they found as many as 100 gold coins each, and taking into account that at auction some of these coins fetched up to £180 each, one can readily appreciate that the stakes were high.

Some will say that this was immoral, or stealing; but stealing from whom? The bulk of the money had originally belonged to the Portuguese merchants and bankers who requested Admiral Cloudesley to carry their specie to England on their behalf. None of these could ever be identified 250 years after the event. The balance, consisting of English guineas, crowns, half-crowns, shillings and sixpences, would have been a mixture of personal and government money, but having been informed of its presence and then declining to take up its option, surely the Government had morally forfeited its rights? Had the state claimed the wreck initially, withdrawn all the contracts, and then used the more than adequate services of the Royal Navy to carry out a full scale salvage operation, then the nation would have benefited by at least a quarter of a million pounds, possibly more. As it was, this sum passed into private hands.

A dream is born

During 1966, the year before the *Association* was relocated, fate decreed that the paths of three men, none of whom had met before, were to cross, and that as a direct result of that meeting, the Scillies would yield the wrecks of two Dutch East India Company ships, about which little or nothing was known locally. Until that year, a London solicitor named Rex Cowan had no interest whatsoever in diving, only a passing interest in treasure hunting, but a passionate interest in the Scillies, the sea and a good story, for he was already a part-time author.

One day, out of sheer curiosity, Rex Cowan went aboard the XSV *Puttenham* at Penzance, the minesweeper used by the *Association* diving team.

Left. *The search for the **Hollandia** led Cowan to Holland, where he examined contemporary accounts of the wreck which had baffled treasure hunters for centuries.*
Above. *Gold buttons, once the property of one of the **Hollandia's** passengers, were a rare find.*

It was there that Cowan met Terry Montgomery, then serving in the Royal Navy as a Commissioned Wardmaster, and a member of the Scillies NAC-SAC diving team. They talked about ships and diving; about treasure and the possibility of finding the sunken warship out on the Gilstone. In the space of a few hours conversation, Rex Cowan became keenly interested.

Little could he have known that this incident would, in time, completely change his way of life, his career, his income, his very being; and at the same time establish his name amongst the successful treasure hunters. Had he been able to look into a crystal ball and foresee the future, he might well have walked away from that ship

and taken up some other interest. As he has since said: 'I would have made more money over the years as a London bus driver'!

The third person to become involved, and to suffer a complete change in life, was Anthony Lonsdale who, along with his brother Bryan, ran an electronics company. He too had no interest in diving; he wasn't keen on the sea at all, since he was almost permanently seasick when afloat – but he *was* interested in treasure, and the application of electronics to new ventures.

Terry Montgomery played only a small part in this episode, since he was to emigrate to Australia on leaving the Navy in 1968. However, he communicated enough enthusiasm to Rex for the latter to take a deep personal interest in the search for the *Association*. Likewise, Anthony Lonsdale played only a small part at that time, but later, when the need for a sophisticated electronic metal detector was apparent, the Lonsdale brothers were to provide and perfect equipment without which the wrecks of the

Hollandia and *Princess Maria* would never have been found.

And so the stage was set, only awaiting the signal for the curtain to rise, this being the location of Sir Cloudesley's flagship, *Association*. When eventually the wreck was located in 1967, Rex Cowan was in an ideal position as a by-stander. Rather like a theatre critic sitting back in his balcony seat, he could observe the entire scene, appreciate the difficulties and mistakes being made, and learn something from them. Had he not had the opportunity and foresight to do this, then many of the same mistakes made on the Gilstone would have been repeated when he, too, set out to find a fortune in the sea.

Ghost ships of the Scillies

The reader may well ask at this point: why was it that no one else was able to take the initiative to research and find the wrecks of the two Dutch East India Company ships with which Rex Cowan's name has become inextricably linked – especially as he was a newcomer to this game? To understand the answer, one must first know something of the long and turbulent history of the Isles of Scilly.

From the year 1337, when right of wreck in the islands reverted from the church to the crown, and the Black Prince was endowed with the Duchy of Cornwall, there should have been royal and, hence in theory, absolute control over all wreck incidents in the Scillies. In practice there was very little control at all, due mainly to the sheer isolation of the islands which, apart from their separation from the mainland, were some five days from London by horse.

In fact, in the majority of shipping incidents, it was the locals who benefited at the expense of the crown, but only if the wreck was of little value. Should anything bigger, or more valuable be at stake, then the authorities would attempt to seize the same for their masters. In this task they were aided, from 1536 onwards, by the newly appointed Vice-Admiral for Devon and Cornwall and, from 1571, by successive

Below. *One of the more surprising finds from the* **Hollandia** *was this snuff-box, the lid of which is decorated with a satire on the Pope.*
Right. *It is coins, above all, which the treasure hunter hopes to find. For this reason, the* **Hollandia,** *which left Holland carrying 129,000 guilders, was a highly attractive proposition.*

members of the Godolphin family, who leased the islands. Since the only record of wreck was that in letters and other correspondence between the tenant and the crown, it was possible to arrange that all documentary evidence was destroyed, or never made public, should the need arise.

During the period 1641-1743, it is now known that a total of seven ships, which can truthfully be classified as 'treasure ships', were lost in or around the Isles of Scilly. Of these seven, three of them, namely the *Association, Romney* and *Eagle,* have already received mention; only the latter remaining to be found at some future date. Very little documentation concerning these losses exists, other than the death notices of Sir Cloudesley Shovell. Not one reference has been found relating to salvage at the time, or the results of Deputy Paymaster Herbert's expedition to the islands to recover the 'Queen's plate' in 1709.

Of the remaining four ships, the richly laden *Triumph,* wrecked on Steval Rock, St Marys, on 9 October 1736, is well documented, and it is known she was heavily salvaged. Homeward bound from Jamaica to London with rum, sugar, dyewood and other cargo, she also carried £10,000 in gold coin. Fortunately for her owners, she went ashore only a stone's throw from the Garrison, which offered full protection until the specie had been recovered.

Royal plunder

Only three treasure ships remain, and it is remarkable that they have managed to retain their obscurity over the years. The 700 ton *Merchant Royal* was the first of these to be lost, being 'cast away when ten leagues from Lands End', on 23 September 1641. Armed with 36 bronze cannon, and carrying a crew of 80, with a few passengers in addition, under the command of Captain John Timby, she also had on board the sum of '£300,000 in silver, £100,000 in gold, and as much again in jewel'. Her sinking was witnessed by another vessel in company, who informed the authorities on arrival at Plymouth that there had been no survivors. The incident was of sufficient importance for Samuel

*Left. Visual searches conducted from a boat were tiring and usually unrewarding. It was not until the diving team acquired a magnetometer that the wreck of the **Hollandia** was located.*

Pepys to interrupt the proceedings of the House of Commons in order to make the sad announcement. It is difficult to estimate the possible current value of this vast amount of treasure still on the sea-bed, but certainly it must be in excess of £2 million.

Next, in order of sinking, was the Dutch East Indiaman *Princess Maria,* lost amongst the Western Rocks in February 1686, the exact date not being known. There is probably only one reference in this country to her loss, despite the fact she was the largest vessel ever built for the Dutch East India Company, and carried a vast amount of silver when she was wrecked. This one reference, in the Calendar of State Papers (Domestic), makes mention of 'the *Princess,* a Dutch vessel, cast away in Cornwall', and it would appear that the writer of the letter in question did not know her full name.

There is evidence to suggest that all references to the wreck were deliberately destroyed on the instructions of King James II, who in fact had stolen the bulk of the treasure from the wreck and had it shipped back to London aboard his own private yacht, the *Isabella.* In the archives of the Rix Museum, at the Hague, there are literally hundreds of references to the wreck, including details of James II's dubious actions, and of the attempts to salvage her for the company; but in England it was as if the wreck never existed.

Wreck of the *Hollandia*

Last of all was the *Hollandia,* which had also faded into obscurity, despite the fact she was not lost until 1743 – only two hundred and thirty years ago. A full account of her loss, one of the few references to the incident in this country, is contained in a booklet entitled 'A Natural and Historical Account of the Isles of Scilly', written by Robert Heath, in about 1750. This reads: 'About the year 1743, a Dutch East Indiaman, outward bound, was lost off St Agnes in about twenty or twenty-two fathoms of water, with all the people. Their firing of guns, as a signal of their distress, was heard in the night; but none could give them assistance. Many of their bodies floated ashore at St Marys and other islands, where they were buried by the inhabitants, and some were taken up floating upon the tide and were buried. A Dutch lady with her children and servants, going to her husband, an East India Governor, was prevented seeing of him by this unhappy accident. A diver thereupon was sent by the Dutch Merchants to discover and weigh the Plate of considerable value. But the tide running strong at bottom, and the sea appearing thick, the diver could not see distinctly through the glass of his engine, so returned without success. This wreck remains a Booty for those who can find it'.

The intriguing part about Heath's reference is not the details of the actual loss, which have since proved to be perfectly correct, but the complete lack of detail as to the vessel's identity, or date of her sinking. At the time he wrote his account, Heath was a Lieutenant in the Garrison, and therefore in a position of some authority. Surely he would have been able to establish the name of the wreck, along with the date of loss, even if only to get the facts correct in his manuscript. After all, the incident had only occurred seven years previously.

Literally thousands of people have read Heath's account of this wreck, but of all these, only one person, Rex Cowan, believed in it sufficiently to make further investigations. As a direct result of research carried out in Holland, by both Rex and his very capable wife, Zelide, they uncovered not only the name *Hollandia*, which was, of course, Heath's wreck, but also that of the *Princess Maria*, and relevant connections with Jacob Johnson and Lethbridge.

Hollandia's last voyage

The *Hollandia* was built in 1742, at Amsterdam, and was therefore on her maiden voyage when she sailed from the Texel for Batavia, on 3 July 1743. Of 700 tons displacement, and measuring 150 Amsterdam feet in length, (1 Amsterdam foot × 28cm = 11.25in), she was commanded by Captain Jan Kelder, who had the responsibility of 276 crew and soldiers and 30 passengers – including the brother of Gustaff Willem Baron Van Imhoff, the Governor General of the Dutch East Indies, with his wife, children, and sister-in-law, who was married to the Baron.

Captain Kelder also had charge of 129,700 guilders, being taken to the Far East in order to allow the Company to purchase trade goods for the return voyage, as was the practice at the time.

Hollandia left Holland in company with two other ships, both of which successfully completed their voyage, but ten days after leaving port, having safely navigated the

Above. *Sceptics claimed that cannon could not survive in the rough seas round the Scillies – Cowan's discoveries proved them wrong.*

Shetland Isles and west coast of Ireland, she struck the Gunner Rock in Broad Sound during the early hours of 13 July. What followed will never be known for certain since, as Lieutenant Heath related, 'she was lost with all the people'. It can only be presumed that she commenced to fill with water after starting leaks, and attempted to reach St Agnes light, but sank in 100 feet of water, 1½ miles east of the Gunner, on George Peters Ledge, before help could reach them.

Despite the fact that the Dutch East India Company were quite used to losing a considerable number of their ships, along with the valuable silver they almost always carried, in this instance they made considerable efforts to recover their property. 'If we lose five or six ships a year, then this represents only five or six per cent' was the attitude of the Company, but in this case they hired the services of Lethbridge to find the wreck and recover the money.

When the famous diver arrived in Scilly, or what exactly he achieved, if anything, is not known. All we know is that he returned empty-handed, either having found the wreck but been unable to get inside her, or else not being able to locate her at all. The former is more likely, since Lethbridge knew sufficient about ships on the bottom to know that she would soon be torn to pieces by winter gales, when access to the treasure would be easier. In this case he would have returned another year, and recovered the coins; instead, they remained on the bottom until 1971.

The hunt is on

The actual relocation of the *Association,* and a first hand sighting of the gold and silver coins the divers were recovering, was the stimulus necessary to convince Cowan that he, too, would start his own private treasure hunt. There was now no doubt that old wrecks could survive in exposed areas, and final confirmation appeared in the form of an intact ship's bell, a navigation slate, and a great deal more gold and silver coin

Above. *Restored to its former glory, a cannon from the **Hollandia** clearly shows the initials 'VOC', symbol of the Dutch East India Company.*

from the supposed site of the *Romney,* found on Tearing Ledge, close to the Bishop Rock, and less than a mile from the Gilstone.

It now only remained to ensure that there would be no repetition of the mistakes made over the *Association,* which, basically, were made over the question of ownership. Before Rex Cowan put even one diver in the sea, he went to the Dutch government, told them of his researches, produced proof – on paper – that the wreck really existed, and asked for an exclusive contract for the *Hollandia.*

Unfortunately, neither Cowan, nor anyone else knew where the wreck lay, so that the contract granted in the end was not for a particular ship, but rather any Dutch East India Company vessel within a certain designated area of the Scillies. Cowan, therefore, had to take a chance, and declare the particular area in which he thought the *Hollandia* was to be found. A

great deal hung in the balance since, while he had nicely sewn up the area in question, and agreed that the Dutch, in return, could have 25 per cent of all items proven to be Dutch Government property, a rival in the Scillies had also staked a claim and sewn up another area.

By now, a number of the Navy diving team were on the point of leaving the service for various reasons, and from them Cowan persuaded Jack Gayton, who had been a Lieutenant Commander, and Nowell Pearce, an ex-Chief Petty Officer, to work for him as divers.

Thinking perhaps that it would not take more than one season to find the *Hollandia,* the divers commenced a visual search of designated areas of the bottom of Broad Sound. This suffered many disadvantages; namely that, if underwater visibility was poor on any day, then the actual area covered by a diver looking for a wreck site was very limited. Also it was impossible to guarantee that the area had been covered completely.

The divers deserve every respect, for day after day, week after week, month after month, they searched and searched – and found nothing. The sea in Broad Sound can be in excess of 150 feet deep in places, which imposes a severe limitation on a diver's 'bottom time' in any one day, and hence slowed the search down considerably. The small team searched the area around Gunner Rock, some of the deeper areas, and then some of the more shallow; and began to realise as the first year drew to a close that, at this rate it could take years to locate the *Hollandia.*

Electronics aid the search

It was at this point that the last member of the trio which had met in Penzance in 1967 came into his own. Anthony Lonsdale was approached and asked to make a suitable metal detector. He produced a proton spin magnetometer, which initially was somewhat crude, but with practice in its operation, and modifications, it was developed into a very sophisticated and sensitive instrument.

Searching for the elusive wreck could now be carried out from the relative comfort of a boat, using divers only to check out indications of

Left. *Set against a painting of Dutch East Indiamen, a hoard of coins from the **Hollandia** indicates the riches recovered in the Scillies.*

metal on the seabed. This gave far greater accuracy when searching predetermined areas, and of course searching could continue all day, every day, provided the weather was reasonable. The team in opposition to Rex Cowan also acquired the use of a magnetometer, and it was not long before two rival boats were sweeping up and down Broad Sound, rather like two minesweepers in wartime, only praying that when the *Hollandia* was found it would be within the area for which they had agreement with the Dutch Government.

It took a great deal of determination, patience and skill to operate the magnetometer day after day, week after week. A few moments lack of concentration, and either the operator would miss the electronic indication showing there was metal on the bottom, or the helmsman would allow the boat to wander off course. In fact it is now certain that the team did in fact pass over the *Hollandia*, obtained a small magnetic reading, put a diver down to investigate, but he probably went off to one side of the wreck, missed the anchors and cannon and surfaced reporting that the bottom was 'clean'.

At a later date, the team went back and re-checked the many small readings they had obtained, since the wreck still eluded them, and this time the reading was stronger. A diver went down to look at the bottom and surfaced with the exciting news that there was a great mass of cannon, several great anchors, bronze cannon; and they bore the famous VOC mark, which signified the Dutch East India Company. The date was 16 September 1971, and the *Hollandia* had been found.

There was only one complication, the wreck was not inside the area contracted from the Dutch, so Rex Cowan had to make a further visit to Holland to get a completely watertight contract for the wreck itself. This gave the team sole rights to work the wreck, with 25 per cent of the gross proceeds of everything going to the Dutch: everything, that is, which could be proven to have once belonged to the Dutch East India Company. Small personal and unmarked items would be treated as wreck within the law of Britain, and hence sold at public auction after the requisite period of one year and a day.

A massive hoard of silver

Whilst the team wanted to carry out an unhurried excavation and survey of the site, it was obvious that as long as the silver remained on the sea-bed it would be a temptation, if not an invitation, for someone to attempt to steal. The area in which the coin was located was quite small, perhaps the size of a large dining table, but in order to salvage them undamaged, they had to be chipped out from the concretion surrounding everything on the wreck. Although the location was kept secret for some weeks, it was not long before news of the find leaked out and diving teams began to salvage the wreck illegally. It was here that Cowan's past experience of the law was an asset and, unlike the case of the *Association*, where there was no exclusive contract, it was possible to take anyone to court who attempted to loot the *Hollandia*.

In order to recover the bulk of the treasure before the bad weather set in for the winter, the diving team was increased from two to four; so with a maximum time of 30 minutes underwater, the diver's working day was relatively short.

The one aspect of the *Hollandia* which made it quite unique, was that it was completely virgin, having remained untouched since the day it sank. She was a 'time capsule' in the truest sense of the term, since she sank carrying all the daily utensils, equipment, clothing, weapons, tools and accoutrements of the mid 1750's, and they were all trapped in one place.

Very little of the *Hollandia's* timbers remained, but otherwise almost everything was found intact. There was no telling what would be found next when the divers dug deep into the sand and black concretion. It might be a bronze gun, or a gold finger ring; a pewter plate, or a silver coin. Strangely enough, not a single gold coin was found aboard; only thousands and thousands of silver cobs, pillar eight reales, ducatons and four, two, and one reale pieces. The hammered cobs, from Spanish South America, have a fascinating background, since the silver from which they were minted was probably mined in Lima or Potosi, in Peru, and was then pack-muled across the mountains to Nombre di Dios or Vera Cruz, where it would be loaded aboard one of the Spanish Plate Fleet ships, to be landed at Cadiz or Vigo to swell the coffers of Phillip V of Spain.

Right. *Perhaps the finest artefact recovered from the* **Hollandia** *was this military mortar, now housed in a Dutch museum.*

Left. *A diver secures lifting tackle to a cannon from the **Princess Maria** – the most recent wreck discovery in the Scillies.*

Above. *Hardly marked by over two centuries under the sea, pieces of eight from mints in Peru flank a silvery rider.*

Whilst one can be romantic about treasure hunting, it has to be financed like any other venture – at least until something of value is found. In the case of the *Hollandia,* an auction of coins and artefacts was held at Sothebys on 18 April 1972. At this sale, 484 lots of coins were offered, with a further ten lots of such items as pewter spoons, plates, sets of wooden knives and the like. This was followed by another summers work, then a sale in New York; more work and a sale at Penzance in July 1973, and another at the same place in late September. It was at this last sale that a fine, bronze Dutch military mortar was offered for sale. It was one of a pair, the other having been purchased by the Dutch Government and taken back to Holland on a warship a few weeks previous. The piece fetched £2,500.

Although publicity was concentrated on Rex Cowan and his team, and the masses of coin

they continued to raise, there were moments when the attention shifted. In 1969, for example, a bronze cannon was found on the *Association* site, and proved to be the most valuable recovered to date. Highly ornamented and marked with the date of its casting, 1604, it sold for £5,000. A chance find of a pocket of silver coins was made in 1973 on the Gilstone site, and a final count revealed that 7,000 English crowns, half-crowns and shillings had been recovered; and this from a site on which hundreds of divers had literally spent thousands of hours. It is not an exaggeration to say that silver coins will still be found there for years to come.

Another wreck discovered

Having found the *Hollandia* and recovered the bulk of the material on the bottom, the diving team was left alone to carry on while another magnetometer search was conducted for the next Indiaman, the *Princess Maria.* The chosen leader of this new team was another Navy man, who also had experience on the Gilstone site. This was Roy Graham, an ex-Lieutenant who had settled in the Scillies on retirement, and had elected to take part in this interesting project.

Unlike the *Hollandia,* there was not even one

clue as to where the wreck might lie; and apart from the realistic assumption that she lay somewhere amongst the Western Rocks, or else in Broad Sound, there was nothing to do but start searching an area which had already been thoroughly surveyed.

By this time, the magnetometer had reached a high pitch in development and hence the second team had the advantage of an experienced operator and better equipment. They needed both, since they had no idea where the *PM*, as the wreck became known, was going to be found. As with the previous team, they searched and searched, first in deep water, then shallow. They discovered more wreck sites than anyone knew existed in the Western Rocks, but none of them was *the* wreck. A good metallic response in 130 feet of water raised their hopes one day, but a diving survey showed it was none other than the remains of HMS *Firebrand,* one of the vessels lost the same night as the *Association.*

Finally, in late summer, 1973, the remains of the *Princess Maria* were located. Obviously it is not ethical at this early stage to disclose any details of the site, other than to say that it is amongst the Western Rocks. She lies in much shallower water than the *Hollandia,* so that working the site does not present any real problems of decompression. In this instance, although the *Princess Maria* sank 57 years prior to the other Indiaman, huge sections of the vessel's deck timbers are still intact beneath the sand. A great many items have been recovered which prove, beyond any doubt, that this is the vessel in question. It will probably take two years of excavation and survey to completely excavate the site.

Certainly the second team were lucky in that they had the advantage of better equipment, no tedious visual searching to do in deep water, and information passed on as to where the wreck *wasn't* situated; but their trump card was the contract given them by the Dutch Government. This gave them exclusive rights to the *Princess Maria,* even if someone else found it first.

Looking to the future
The Isles of Scilly will continue to yield coins

Left. *A diver combs the sea-bed round the site of the* **Hollandia.** *It is likely that the wrecks discovered in the Scillies will continue to yield treasures for many years to come.*

and valuable artefacts from the five wrecks mentioned for many years to come and, long after the professionals have completed their work, amateurs will find bits and pieces for themselves. In time, someone will locate the wreck of HMS *Eagle*, and possibly the *Merchant Royal*. But neither of them will be easy, for they are almost certainly in deep water, inaccessible to present day divers unless costly and advanced diving equipment is available. By that time the law of salvage will have changed, and perhaps the salvors will enjoy a measure of protection, and receive a better financial reward for their initiative.

If anything good has come out of the treasure wrecks found amongst the Scillies, it is the 1973 Bill for the Protection of Historic Wrecks, designed to protect wrecks of historic, archaeological or other value and which lie in United Kingdom waters. In effect, the area round such a wreck can be designated a 'restricted area', and the would-be visitor must obtain a licence from the Secretary of State before he can enter this area. Licences may be granted for many legitimate purposes, but may restrict or forbid certain activities – such as removing objects or otherwise tampering with a wreck. Offences against the Act may be punishable by an unlimited fine – a powerful deterrent to the casual 'treasure hunter'.

The benefits of this legislation are obvious. Only responsible and qualified researchers will be allowed to work a site and squalid competition between teams is avoided. Most important; in the event of treasure being recovered, it will be recovered entire and can be sold, or otherwise disposed of, as a collection. Conceivably, we may yet see the foundation of a museum devoted entirely to underwater finds. Such a collection would add immeasurably to our knowledge of history – in particular the marine history which is so much a part of Britain's past.

Below. *A hoard of precious coins newly recovered from the wreck of the* **Hollandia.** **Right.** *An interesting find from the* **Princess Maria** *was this corked Bellarmine flagon filled with 40lb of mercury.*

TREASURE ISLAND BRITAIN

Edward Fletcher

Buried treasure worth more than £10,000,000 was found in Britain between 1900 and 1970, a total reached by the accidental discovery of approximately half a dozen hoards every year. If such discoveries were to continue at the same rate, their value would probably reach £20,000,000 before the end of the century. It now seems likely, however, that modern scientific aids will help double even that staggering figure long before the year 2000.

The number of hoards found in 1973 by amateur treasure hunters equipped with metal detectors, was greater than the number found by farm workers and building site labourers who, until 1972, regularly topped the league of treasure finders. True, the farmers and labourers retained their position as recoverers of the richest finds; but as metal detecting equipment becomes more sophisticated, and the number of people hunting buried treasure with electronic aids increases, finds made by deliberate search must soon overhaul finds made by accident.

Below. *Richest of all treasure finds in Britain, these dishes from the Mildenhall hoard are a superb example of Roman art.*

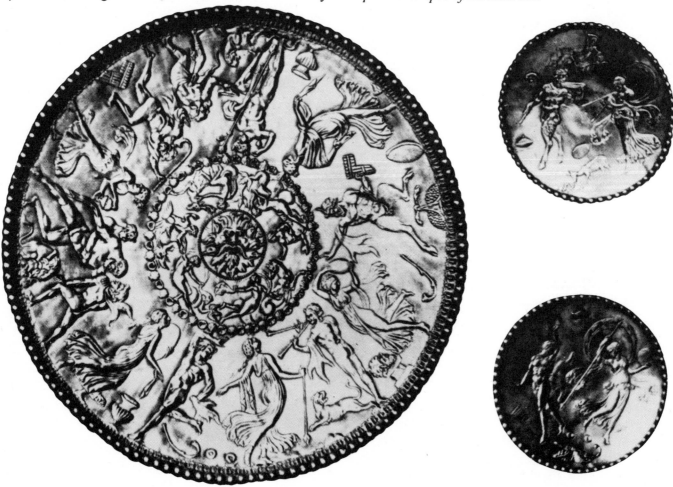

The richest treasure found in Britain during this century was discovered by tractor driver Gordon Butcher in a lonely Suffolk field in February 1940. Butcher was ploughing a four-acre plot on Thistly Green, on the outskirts of Mildenhall, when his ploughshare struck buried metal. He stepped down from the tractor to investigate damage to his machine and uncovered with his bare hands a Third Century Romano-British silver dish measuring over two feet in diameter. Later that day, Butcher and his employer, Arthur Ford, dug out the dish and found another 32 unique pieces of silverware hidden beneath it. The entire hoard – the Mildenhall Treasure – is now exhibited in the British Museum. Conservative estimates put its present value at more than £2,000,000.

Butcher was not the only man to find buried treasure in that eventful year of 1940, when the Royal Air Force took on the might of Hitler's Luftwaffe in the skies above Britain. During the

Above. *The Mildenhall treasure is valued at £2,000,000 and is made up of 32 pieces of beautifully engraved silverware.*

same week in which Butcher made his find, a man in Cobham, Kent discovered a hoard of gold sovereigns in the hollow leg of a chest-of-drawers; and in August, a coroner holding a Treasure Trove inquest in Hampshire remarked that it was the second inquest he had held that year. He went on to say that 50 Treasure Trove inquests had been held in England alone during the 14 years up to 1940. When figures for Scotland, Wales and Northern Ireland are added, they show that the average of six hoards per year for the whole of Great Britain was surpassed in this period. It may be that the Government's war-time exhortation to 'Dig for Victory' caused the increase.

The particular treasure find on which the Hampshire coroner was holding his inquest

when he gave these figures, occurred in the village of Freefolk, when workmen, repairing an old cottage on the farm estate owned by Lord Portal, found an earthenware jar containing 358 sovereigns. Within an hour of the first jar coming to light a second was unearthed. It held 254 half-sovereigns. When numismatists inspected the finds, they were able to say that both jars must have been buried after 1876, the latest date on any of the coins.

Riches from the ground

The discovery of two hoards buried in close proximity like this is a constantly recurring theme in the story of buried treasure. Those who hope to find hidden riches have a far greater chance of turning up a fortune if they concentrate their searches around spots where one hoard has already been located. Proof of this rule has come from every county in Britain, but none of the finds demonstrated this truth more dramatically than one made in Essex in 1969.

It was in February of that year that George Purvis, a workman on a building site in Colchester, dug up an ancient lead casket while cutting a trench on the site of an old chemist's shop. His pick knocked the top off the container and Mr. Purvis found himself gazing down on a sparkling hoard of 10,000 silver coins. They were in such fine condition that at first Mr. Purvis thought he had found a hoard of modern sixpences; but later inspection revealed they were 13th century long-cross pennies, worth up to £50 each. Several days later, when officials at the local museum were checking records on the history of the site, it was learned that in 1920, a lead bucket containing 11,000 short-cross pennies had been found a few feet from the spot on which Mr. Purvis made his discovery.

· Less than two years were to elapse between Mr. Purvis' windfall and the next spectacular find on a known treasure site. On this occasion it was the residents of Holcolme Crescent, Ipswich who were to learn that treasure hunting history usually repeats itself on the same spot. When the houses in Holcolme Crescent were being built in 1968, a bulldozer driver dug up five gold torcs during earthmoving operations. The torcs – Celtic necklaces worn by British

Left. *2,000 years after it was thrown into the Thames as a last gesture to its warrior owner, the Battersea shield was recovered, unmarked.*

chieftains – went to the British Museum and their finder received a Treasure Trove reward of £45,000. No doubt the new neighbours of Holcolme Crescent found the torcs an interesting topic of conversation during their house-warming parties later that year; but it was not until one resident, Mr Peter Gorham, got down to the task of digging his new garden in October 1970 and turned up a sixth torc on the end of his fork that the entire neighbourhood caught 'torc-fever'. Frantic horticultural activity followed, but no more torcs were found. Nevertheless, when a house in Holcolme Crescent is sold nowadays, it is always pointed out to the prospective purchaser that the garden might hold more than flowers. Residents who have done their treasure hunting homework can also remind sceptics that in 1907, nine Celtic gold bracelets were found at Crayford, Kent – on a spot where eight others had been found one year earlier – and that gold torcs have also been found in gardens in Norfolk, Somerset and Cambridgeshire.

Treasure gardens

Indeed, gardens have proved time and again to hold rich treasures. In April 1901, two little girls playing in the marshland village of Luddington, near Goole, Lincolnshire, accidentally threw their ball into a garden. When they went to retrieve it they picked up a guinea piece lying on top of the soil in a flower-bed. They took it home to their mother who returned with them to the site, which adjoined a derelict house. Within a few minutes the woman found another forty coins – all dated 1774 – and news of her finds spread like wildfire through the village. Soon the entire population was digging frantically. Hundreds of guineas were found in the overgrown garden before the local constable appeared to disperse the mob and claim those coins he managed to retrieve as Treasure Trove.

Nine years later, in March 1910, another village constable in Winterslow, Wiltshire, was more fortunate. He had arranged to have some building work carried out in his own garden and had called in a local contractor named Yates to do the work. As the constable looked on, Yates began to dig a trench across the lawn. At a depth of 18 inches his spade struck an earthenware jar, which he and the policeman carefully lifted out of the hole. When opened, it was found to contain a hoard of silver coins covering the reigns of Mary and Philip, Edward VI, Elizabeth I, Charles I and James I. The constable took charge and the entire hoard was later declared Treasure Trove.

In November of the same year, another interesting find was made in the garden of Sunlaws House, near Kelso. One of the servants was clearing a mound of garden refuse when he discovered a chest containing a large amount of valuable jewellery. At the subsequent Treasure Trove inquest, the owner of Sunlaws House, Colonel Scott Kerr, gave evidence that twenty-five years earlier, Sunlaws House had been burned to the ground. Before rebuilding commenced, those personal possessions of the household destroyed by the fire were dumped in the rear garden. Colonel Scott Kerr thought it possible that the chest of jewels had belonged to his deceased mother and that it had been thrown out by accident after the fire. The coroner agreed with him and the chest was returned to the colonel.

The year 1932 was another vintage one for garden treasures; the two largest hoards found that year both turned up in jars buried in gardens. On 9 November, Allan Wilson of Elizabeth Street, Elland, Yorkshire, dug up the first in his cabbage patch. It contained 1,807 silver coins dated 1520-1605. Ten days later another gardener in Fish Lane, Selsey, unearthed 1,000 Roman silver coins in an urn found two feet beneath his late potato crop.

More recently, in June 1960, Mr. J. Allen of Longton, near Stoke-on-Trent, was digging a trench in his garden when he found a Roman jar containing over 2,000 coins. A boy aged four struck gold in his garden at Winston Avenue, Tadleigh, near Basingstoke, when he found a rusty tin beneath a pear tree. It contained 21 golden guineas and half-guineas of George III's reign.

The lure of gold

It is gold and tales of its finding that make the pulses of hopeful treasure hunters race. However large or valuable a hoard turns out to be, there is always a sense of anti-climax if it does not include the noble metal; and it is finds of hidden gold in Britain which always arouse the greatest public interest. In July 1971, for instance, when a hoard of 9,000 silver coins valued at £200,000 was sold at Spinks, the affair created little enthusiasm outside the numismatic

circles; in spite of the fact that the coins were genuine pirate treasure found in only ten feet of water off a popular beach in the Caribbean. A few weeks later, firemen who fought a blaze in a derelict cottage at Wymington, Bedfordshire found a metal box stuffed with gold sovereigns and other coins. The value of the treasure was insignificant when compared to that of the pirate's booty, yet because some of the coins were gold and they had been found in our own treasure island, the event was widely reported in the popular press.

Another golden treasure find which most people in Britain enjoyed reading about in their morning papers, occurred in March 1966, when Mr John Craughwell of Nottingham dug up a hoard of more than 1,000 medieval gold coins near Newstead Abbey. He was driving a mechanical trench-digger at the time, and when the teeth of the bucket bit into the ground a

cascade of coins fell from the walls of the trench. Mr Craughwell and his workmates scrambled into the hole and began stuffing coins into their pockets as fast as they could. Later, when the digger driver counted and weighed the contents of his pockets at home, he found that he had picked up 348 coins and that they weighed over five pounds. It was then that he realized they must be gold and he hurriedly took them to the local police station. When his fellow workers handed their spoils in, the hoard was found to include a gold cross with a ruby inset, three rings, a brooch and a gold chain. Many of the coins were gold nobles and some were dated 1199. A British Museum official said later: "This is the largest hoard of gold coins from this period found in Britain since 1939".

The hoard of pre-Roman gold and tin coins found in a field at Snettisham, Norfolk, in December 1948, was considerably smaller; but the entire Snettisham Treasure, found during a period of several weeks, was yet another priceless discovery made by farmers. The story began in the first week of December when a ploughman turned up three oddly shaped ob-

Below. *Metal detector users make their richest pickings on old battlegrounds – Cromwellian ball and shot are a common find.*

jects in the field. After inspecting his finds briefly, he discarded them on the edge of the field as worthless hunks of iron and returned to his work. Some days later a second hoard of metal was discovered. It contained the broken pieces of ten gold torcs, together with several items of bronze jewellery and a number of tin coins. A hurried search was made for the three 'hunks of worthless iron' around the edge of the field, and the glint of gold was seen when they

Above. *A policeman holds up a gold torc. Torcs were part of the ceremonial regalia of a Celtic chieftain and were credited with mystic powers.*

were inspected closely. They, too, were gold torcs; the largest measured nine inches in diameter.

At this point, a local archaeologist was called in and it was as he inspected the area around the hole from which the second hoard had come that the next discovery was made. A few feet away a third hoard was uncovered. It contained 70 extremely rare tin coins, later dated to 85-87 B.C. The treasures found were undoubtedly the richest ever to come from Norfolk soil; but the final total had yet to be reached. In the last week of December, a hoard of gold and tin coins turned up – proving once again that treasure is most likely to be discovered in those places where it has already been found.

Finds in houses

Records prove beyond doubt that fields and gardens have held most of the buried treasure found in Britain in the past. Nevertheless, some exciting finds have also been made in houses. There was an unexpected windfall for a lady in Princes Avenue, Hull, who decided to sweep a bedroom chimney in the Spring of 1946. When she pushed the brush up the flue, out fell a biscuit tin containing £600 in notes. In the same year, a man in Newcastle-under-Lyme found a stocking filled with gold coins and notes worth £500 when he took up floorboards in the

Below. *The Snettisham treasure, of which this torc is a part, was at first discarded by its finder, who thought it was useless scrap metal.*

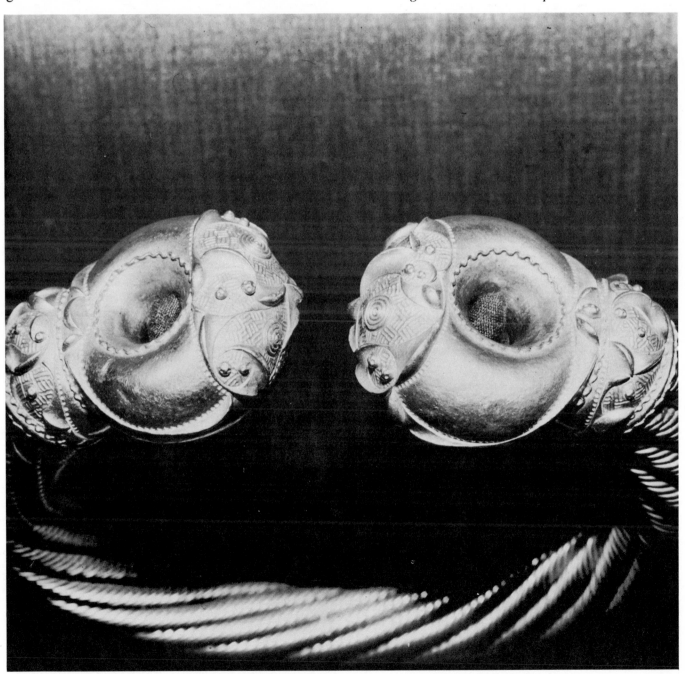

bedroom of his house. Another do-it-yourself enthusiast in Winshill, near Burton-on-Trent, who removed floorboards at his home in November 1960, found silver coins worth £400 hidden there; and an even bigger find was discovered beneath floorboards in January 1944. It was uncovered by a young electrician working in a house at West Hill, Wandsworth, London. He found, between the joists, 1,395 bank-notes, together with 84 sovereigns, 33 half-sovereigns, a box of jewellery and several gold watches. Hoards hidden in houses have also turned up behind loose brickwork, in lavatory cisterns, in gas pipes and under kitchen sinks; but mattresses, teapots and grandfather clocks have consistently proved most popular for the hiding of family fortunes.

The prize for the largest number of coins found at one time in the present century, must go to the workmen who unearthed the Dorchester Treasure in May 1936. There were more than 20,000 coins in the hoard and three containers – a bronze-bound box, an urn and a bowl – were used to hold them. Thirty years earlier, in April 1906, 7,000 coins were found in a single jar which had been ploughed up by a farmer in Stanley, Yorkshire. Several thousand coins were also found together in a field at Llamgarron, in Wales during the Spring of 1914. They had been hurriedly deposited in a shallow hole and a flat stone had been placed over them. A number of other hoard sites have produced more than 4,000 coins – Richborough Castle (8,500); Portishead, Somerset (4,100); Preston, Dorset (4,500); Hollingbourne, Kent (5,000); Rockbourne, Hampshire (7,700); and others. All of these finds, and most of the hundred or so which have contained more than 2,000 coins, date from the Roman period. Later hoards are usually smaller and contain up to 500 coins. There have, however, been notable exceptions, including 1,200 silver pennies of Edward I, Edward II and Edward III, found during the building of a police station at Whittonstall, Northumberland in 1958; 1,000 silver pennies dated 1150-1250 found under a stone at Corosin, Co. Clare in 1943 by a six-year-old child; and

Right. *This mysterious head, of some unknown Celtic deity, is mounted on a bronze bucket found at Aylesford, Kent. Its head-dress seems to echo the style found in Egyptian and other early cultures.*

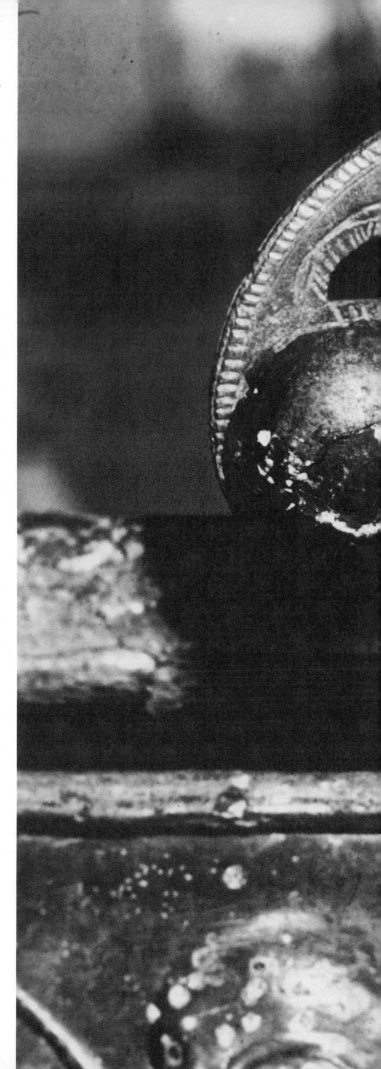

4,000 coins of Edward III, found by a workman at Warminster, Wiltshire, in 1935. Although most medieval hoards contain fewer coins, they are far more valuable than the larger fortunes buried by the Romans.

A growing hobby

Metal detector finds of recent years pale to insignificance when set against the hundreds of thousands of rare coins discovered during ploughing and trench digging operations this century. Most detector finds have been minihoards; Victorian purses containing three or four sovereigns; a pickpocket's cache of rings and watches hidden under a tree; or single gold and silver coins lost in parks and on commons. The reason why so few large hoards have been found by metal-detector users in the three years during which amateur treasure hunting has grown into a popular hobby, is that most of its 30,000 devotees have spent their time coin-shooting – seeking single coins and items of jewellery accidentally lost in public places, such as picnic spots and fairgrounds. Success at this level of treasure hunting is guaranteed, no matter how inexperienced the detector user happens to be. So many coins and items of jewellery have been lost on these sites (official statistics reveal that 180,000,000 coins disappear from circulation every year), that an absolute

Above. An assortment of objects located with the aid of a metal detector. In a single day, the user may find a collection of objects ranging from a rare early Roman coin to a few rusty old bottle tops.

Right. Bottles may seem unlikely treasure, but these Codds are rather rare and valuable.

beginner at coin-shooting has no difficulty in finding 50 in a single day.

Hoard hunting, on the other hand, carries no guarantee of immediate success and only a small minority of detector owners have so far turned their attention to the subject. Many are deterred by lack of time to investigate potential hoard sites thoroughly; research can take up hundreds of hours spent in reading old reports, checking maps, and selecting areas to be searched. If the site is a farmer's field, the detector owner must also be prepared to wait for months until crops are harvested so that he can survey the ground correctly. More often than not, searches must be carried out during winter months when most amateur treasure hunters prefer a comfortable armchair to the rain, wind and snow of a British winter.

Yet in spite of all the difficulties, a dedicated few *are* beginning to make their presence felt. The first major detector find was made by Barrie Thomson of Long Crendon, Buckinghamshire, who located the Grove Wood

Treasure – a hoard of rare Anglo-Saxon coins – in a copse beside the A40, in 1971. He later received a Treasure Trove reward of £8,000. Other detector successes have followed – 5,000 Roman coins found in Sussex; £10,000 in banknotes wrapped in tinfoil located in Essex; a hoard of 18th century silverware discovered on Hampstead Heath; a brass telescope stuffed with gold sovereigns, unearthed in a wood on the outskirts of London – and several more. It is detector finds like these which are convincing a growing number of amateur treasure hunters that hoard research can pay dividends. There seems little doubt that a major treasure – perhaps even more spectacular than the Mildenhall find – will soon be pinpointed with the aid of modern electronics.

The law of Treasure Trove

In spite of the many buried treasures discovered in Britain every year, there is much confusion in the minds of the general public about the laws of Treasure Trove. Many farm hands and building workers believe employers, or the owners of land on which a treasure is found, can claim it even if they were not party to its finding. In fact it is the person who actually finds a treasure who benefits most – *if he acts promptly and in accordance with the laws.* The procedure is straightforward. If you find a hoard, or even a single object of gold, silver, or electrum (the alloy of gold and silver), you must immediately report the fact at a police station or a museum and ensure that your name is recorded as the finder. The police or a museum official will take charge of the find until a Treasure Trove inquest is arranged by the local coroner. At the inquest the coroner must satisfactorily answer three questions: Who found the hoard; was the find promptly and fully reported; and was it originally hidden with the intention of recovery at a later date? If you reported your find as soon as it was made, and if every object found was declared, the coroner's only task is to decide whether or not the find was hidden by someone who intended to recover it later. In the case of a hoard of coins or a number of gold or silver objects hidden in the same place, he will have little hesitation in deciding that the original owner intended but failed to recover them. Once satisfied on this point, the coroner *must* declare the find to be Treasure Trove and seize it on behalf of the Crown. You, as finder, *must* receive as your reward the full market value of the objects you discovered. The only exception to this rule is that, if no museum wishes to buy

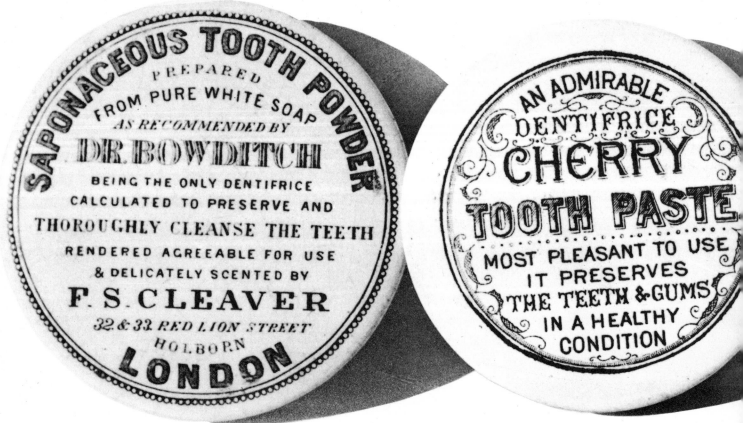

the objects, they must be returned to you to dispose of as you wish. None of the reward or the finds go to your employer or to the owner of the land unless they were directly involved in the finding of the Treasure Trove.

If the coroner cannot decide that the find was buried with the intention of later recovery, he cannot declare it to be Treasure Trove. This could happen in the case of a single object which might have been accidentally lost or used as a religious offering at a sacred shrine. In such a case the coroner would almost certainly return the object to the finder – unless the owner of the land had a better claim. His claim would be strong if you found the object without first asking for permission to search his land.

Below. *Very few treasure hunters can hope to find a hoard as valuable and unique as the riches found at Mildenhall or Snettisham. Increasingly, the amateur treasure hunter concentrates his attention on commonplace objects of an earlier age. Rubbish dumps are particularly rewarding hunting grounds, and the person prepared to work such unsavoury places may be rewarded by the discovery of objects such as these Victorian tooth-paste jars. They make interesting conversation pieces.*

These straightforward rules are worth committing to memory because Treasure Trove can turn up anywhere at anytime. Gordon Butcher, the man who found the Mildenhall Treasure, lost a reward of at least £500,000 because he was ignorant of the Treasure Trove laws. Instead of reporting the find to the police immediately, Butcher told his employer who, after helping the tractor driver to dig up the hoard, took it home and kept it in his house for six years. When these facts eventually came to the ears of the local coroner in 1946, he was unable to satisfy himself that the find had been reported at once. Instead of receiving rewards of £500,000 each, Butcher and Ford were given £1,000 apiece as a token reward in view of the incredible value of the find!

One other story should be memorized by those contemplating a treasure hunt. In January 1966, Terence Davey of Hayling Island, Hampshire, was fishing with his brothers on the island's foreshore, when he found a brass box containing a hoard of 16th century silver coins. Two months later, after several bitter rows with his brothers and Customs and Excise officials over ownership and reward-sharing, he threw the box and its contents back into the sea, declaring as he did so that the day on which he found the treasure was the bitterest day of his life . . .

THE LIEFDE ADVENTURE

Alan Bax

Above. *From the rugged cliffs of Shetland the members of the **Liefde** expedition gaze at the site of the Dutch treasure ship.*

Although there are many interesting and unexplored wrecks around the coasts of the United Kingdom, a good percentage of which warrant marine archaeological survey, and some excavation, very little work had been carried out up to 1965. True, the *Grace Dieu* in the Hamble River had received attention, and some work had been carried out on sunken roads, bridges and buildings in various rivers throughout the country. The famous Tudor warship *Mary Rose*

had also been the subject of an elementary search. However, the only wreck which had drawn any real effort was that of the *Duque di Florencia* in Tobermory Bay, which held the ever-fascinating lure of treasure.

In 1965, the brothers John and Peter Bannon,

proprietors of an Ealing cafe, and their friend Michael Harrison, a cost accountant, saw a television programme concerning the wrecks around Britain, followed later by an article in the Weekend Telegraph on similar lines. As a result they decided to put all their available capital into a treasure-wreck search. There followed a hectic period of research into books and state papers, in order to ascertain which wreck offered the greatest return and the simplest location problem. Things were rather hectic, because it was hoped to get a preliminary expedition away that summer. Finally, despite the distance involved, the wreck of the Dutch East Indiaman *Kennermerlandt* – sometime known as *Carmelan* – lost in the Shetland Islands in 1664, was chosen as the target. All that remained was to find a boat, divers and equipment, and transport them all some 600 miles to the site.

Through the good offices of Mike Borrow, Alan Bax, a Royal Naval Ship Diving Archaeologist was contacted and asked to join the team. Thus treasure hunting was linked with a measure of Marine Archaeology. Soon an expedition was made up, equipment gathered in, and a small boat hired in London. A shortage of suitable boats in Shetland made it impractical to hire one locally within the very tight schedule of the expedition, and so the team had to find a vessel in England. By August all last-minute hitches had been sorted out, and on the 8th, Alan Bax, Malcolm Cavan (an officer from the Attack Swimmers Section of the Royal Marines), Peter Bannon and Mike Harrison sailed from Yarmouth for the Outskerries, Shetland, in search of the *Kennermerlandt*.

Six days later, Cavan dived on the site of a wreck indicated by the Skerry Islanders. He found coins dated 1711. They did not come from the *Kennermerlandt*, but from another East Indiaman – the *Liefde*.

Previous expeditions

Before going on to give the details of the work which has been carried out on the site, it is of interest perhaps to go back over previous expeditions to salvage this vessel. Like *Kennermerlandt*, and all Indiamen, she was an attractive proposition, as considerable quantities of coin, for use as wages, and to replenish the company's coffers, were a normal part of her cargo. She also carried valuable bronze cannon.

The first attempt at recovery certainly seems to have been motivated by the possibility of large amounts of coin, and both professional Dutch salvagemen and Shetland amateurs were competing on the wreck immediately after the disaster. The Dutchman, Luijtje Bontchoe reported in April 1712 that he found only rigging, and Wylie Wybrants stated in May that 'he was unable to fish anything out'. It would seem, therefore, that either the Shetlanders were too 'canny' for their Dutch rivals, or that there was some collusion – all to the detriment of the Dutch East India Company; because at some time that year four Shetlanders are reported as having recovered chests of gold valued at £30,000!

It seems likely that this money was recovered in the winter soon after the disaster, when some part of the wreck was above or very near the sea surface. The two clefts (called 'geos' in Shetland) in the area are known as the 'Dragging Geos' as it is from here that the gold is said to have been 'dragged' out. However, the local salvors did not enjoy every penny of their hard-earned booty. Life, and for that matter the law, changes little, for the Shetlanders on admitting their recovery to the local Crown Official received 30 per cent of its value, from which they had to pay their own salvage expenses!

The next Expedition took place between 1729 and 1735, when a London diver worked on the wrecks of both the *Liefde* and the *Kennermerlandt*. Again he was after treasure, and is said to have recovered some 2,000 ducatoons and 160 ducats. This sees a small sum for so long a labour, however bad the weather and however primitive his equipment must have been; but then this is only what he declared . . .

For some 229 years the wreck then remained untouched by man; but in 1964, when HMS *Shoulton* visited the site, it was found that the forces of nature had taken their toll. A search of the area revealed only two silver ducatoons (which were presented to the Lerwick Museum) and, much more important, a cannon. Time did not permit the *Shoulton* divers to raise the cannon, although an attempt was made.

The actual lifting was carried out by Mr Eric Giles, his wife and two colleagues, who came to dive on the site after the *Shoulton* had left. They relocated the cannon, and towards the end of their holiday enlisted the services of *Snowdrop* – one of the three Skerry fishing vessels – to bring

it to the surface. The cannon was subsequently transported to the Museum at Lerwick.

1965 saw the expedition mentioned initially. Time on the site was only four days, and as the team included two divers only, this permitted only the barest examination which led to the recovery of a small number of coins. It did, however, lead to a great deal of thought over the winter of 1965/66, and another expedition in the summer of 1966.

This expedition, which was staged over a period of eleven days, was led by Alan Bax and included Ian Morrison, a lecturer at Edinburgh University, and Stephen Halliday, a professional underwater photographer. The site was given a basic survey, some tentative rock clearance with the aid of explosive was carried out, and a visual diver search made of an adjacent area. A magnetometer was loaned by Dr E.T. Hall of the Oxford Research Laboratory for Archaeology, and taken to the site; but shortage of time precluded its use.

The 'bonanza' year was in 1967, when two

Above. *Members of the **Liefde** expedition make running repairs to their equipment.*
Fig. 1. *The Shetland Isles are a collection of many small islands – called skerries – each of which is a potential death trap for shipping.*
Bottom right. *The search boat at the wreck site.*

expeditions recovered many artefacts, to say nothing of a chest of silver. First on the scene, in June, was HMS *Delight* on a courtesy visit to Lerwick. By coincidence, Alan Bax was First Lieutenant, and Commander J.M. Child RN permitted the landing of a 24 man team. Elementary lifting methods were tried, and rocks removed from the site which was first broken up by explosives. Further survey work was carried out, and a magnetometer search attempted – results were inconclusive, the errors being more human than electronic. The second expedition worked through August and September. It was led by Owen Gander and financed by the company *Scientific Surveys Ltd.* Some 15 persons took part for periods varying

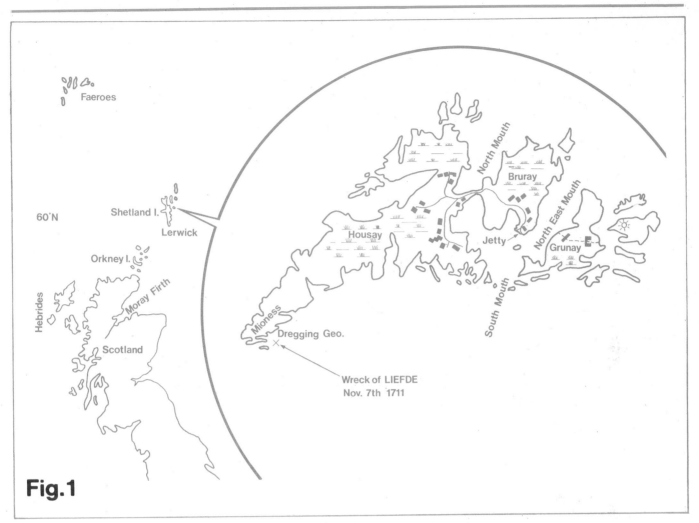

Fig.1

Above. *The 'VOC' insignia, found on objects from the wreck, instantly identify the ship as a Dutch East Indiaman registered in Amsterdam.*

between two weeks and two months. The work involved a great deal of excavation, aided by explosive, the debris being lifted clear by a pontoon and/or airbags.

Finally, in 1969, the most expensive expedition of them all was staged; again financed by *Scientific Surveys*. Work was directed by John Bannon, with on-site work led alternatively by Alan Bax and Owen Gander, backed by Jim Gill throughout.

The ship and her cargo

Laid down in Amsterdam in 1698, *Liefde* was the third ship of that name to be owned by the Dutch East India Company. It would appear that she took some two or three years in building, as her maiden voyage was not until October 1701. She was built for the Holland-Batavia trade, and was on her fourth voyage – each voyage usually lasting two to three years – when she left Texel on her last fateful trip on November 3 1711.

A few particulars of the vessel are of interest;

they are taken from the log of Captain Pronk who commanded the ship during her second voyage, and from the minutes of the 'Gentleman 17' – who were the Directors of the Company.

Captain:	Barent Muijkens (39 years old)
Crew:	200 seamen, 100 soldiers
Length:	150 feet
Beam:	40 feet
Draught:	16 feet
Displacement:	500 tons approx
Anchors:	Weighed between 2,900 and 3,500 pounds
Armament:	10 × Iron 12 pounders
	2 × Bronze 8 pounders
	18 × Iron 8 pounders
	10 smaller guns

The details of her general cargo are not clear, but it is thought that it comprised trading goods and supplies for the Company's staff at the Cape and in Batavia. This theory is born out to an extent by the recovery of over 300 knife handles, a quantity of clay pipe fragments, and some fruit stones which might have formed part of a supply destined to start the fruit farms of the Cape. Almost half her cargo space would have been taken up by beer, water, and goods; stowed as shown in Fig. 3.

The storage of these goods would not have

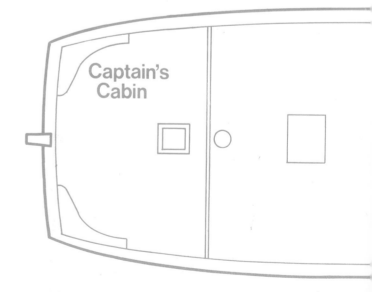

Fig. 3

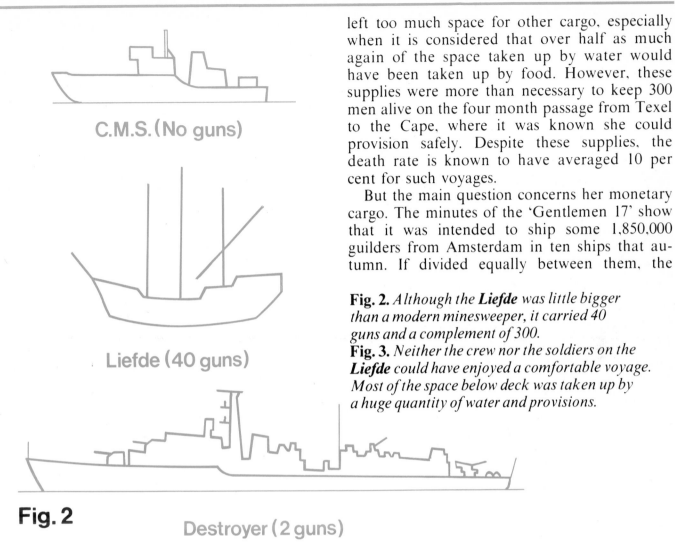

left too much space for other cargo, especially when it is considered that over half as much again of the space taken up by water would have been taken up by food. However, these supplies were more than necessary to keep 300 men alive on the four month passage from Texel to the Cape, where it was known she could provision safely. Despite these supplies, the death rate is known to have averaged 10 per cent for such voyages.

But the main question concerns her monetary cargo. The minutes of the 'Gentlemen 17' show that it was intended to ship some 1,850,000 guilders from Amsterdam in ten ships that autumn. If divided equally between them, the

Fig. 2. *Although the* **Liefde** *was little bigger than a modern minesweeper, it carried 40 guns and a complement of 300.*

Fig. 3. *Neither the crew nor the soldiers on the* **Liefde** *could have enjoyed a comfortable voyage. Most of the space below deck was taken up by a huge quantity of water and provisions.*

C.M.S. (No guns)

Liefde (40 guns)

Fig. 2

Destroyer (2 guns)

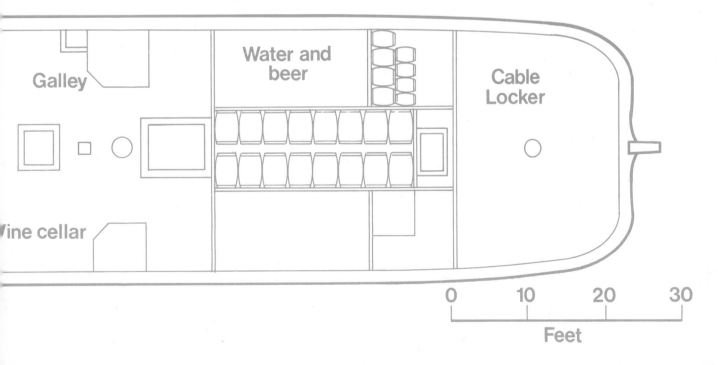

Galley

Water and beer

Cable Locker

Wine cellar

0   10   20   30

Feet

Liefde would have carried a minimum of 185,000 guilders; but she was the largest vessel in the fleet, and records subsequent to the loss quote 227,000 guilders as the replacement figure – which seems a more realistic sum. The total would have been comprised of bars and coin, both gold and silver.

This then was the ship and her cargo. She was heavily armed, mature and well found; but like all vessels of her time she was desperately overcrowded by modern day standards, and the comparisons shown in Fig. 2. are of interest. It is no wonder that a contemporary account (1705) describes the state of the water supply in the following terms: 'The water had to be sucked through clenched teeth to prevent the entrance of crawling vermin'. The modern minesweeper carries water for ten days, the Indiamen enough for four months. In 1711 it would seem that the seaman's lot was not the happiest one ...

The underwater environment

Over four years of diving the average sea temperature at all depths was 52°F. Underwater visibility was seldom less than 30 feet, and was often as much as 50 feet. The seabed in the vicinity of Silver Gulley was a jumble of gneiss boulders, varying in size from about 1 to 250 cubic feet. The jumble extended to the east, but to the west petered out to form a uniform layer of large stones and pebbles between reef and cliff, with a few larger rocks protruding.

The whole area, particularly the reef, cliff face and large boulders, was covered with a thick layer of kelp growing to a height of three to four feet, and extending to a depth of 70 to 80 feet. In this area life abounded – dogfish, lobster and crab, interesting 'sun' starfish, jellyfish, sponge – all watched with curious disinterest by shoals of formation-flying 'tiddlers'.

The water was usually crystal clear in the bottom 10 feet, at lesser depths visibility was often reduced by marine life, including occasional red streaks on the surface. Above water the air temperature seldom exceeded 60°F and was usually in the lower 50's. This low temperature, combined with little sunshine and an apparently high humidity, often made the

Left. *The **Liefde's** bell still bears the first two digits of the date when she was first commissioned in 1701.*

drying of wet gear very difficult; although in 1968 the weather was exceptionally fine throughout.

Winds of up to Force 7 were occasionally experienced, but not for long. Diving was always possible in northerly winds, and it was even possible to dive in southerly winds provided the sea height was not greater than five or six feet. Although such diving was never comfortable – work was carried out 50 feet from a stark lee shore – it was permitted by the provision of a strong four-legged mooring which held the boat stable.

A considerable amount of time was spent underwater through the years, and yet there were no accidents other than a few minor equipment malfunctions. The two main contributory factors to this record were the strict observation of the Royal Navy decompression tables, and the use of experienced divers – though 1968 saw 11 year old Patrick Gill and 15 year old Douglas Yound working on the bottom.

However, there were some special problems associated with the position of the wreck. Again and again warmth, or rather the lack of it, emerged as the limiting factor on a diver's efficiency, above and below water. Although the water was not unduly cold – 50 to 53°F – old 3/16inch wet suits did not permit prolonged static work to be carried out with reasonable efficiency at the working depth of about 48 feet.

When the work was hard physically, and little thought was required, it did not matter quite so much, but as soon as fine detail of thought and action were needed, diver comfort became of paramount importance. The expedition quickly learnt that every effort should be made to ensure that a diver was warm before entering the water, and that cold developed more quickly if he was unable to dry and warm himself after a dive. Heated suits were beyond the means of the expeditions, and so, as an emergency measure, kettles of hot water were poured over the divers in an attempt to maintain body-heat. It was also found that a dry-suit worn over a wet-suit prevented the numbing effects of cold; but this method suffered from a disadvantage in that it restricted movement underwater.

It became clear over the years that the most efficient expedition was one where some 25 to 30 per cent were non-divers. The brunt of the vital work of recording, cataloguing, photographic processing and logging, victualling,

and cylinder charging, was carried out by a standing shore-party, who had no other responsibility, and who were not subject to the rigours of work underwater.

Search methods

Initial location, usually the most difficult problem, was quickly achieved in 1965. However search was and is still necessary to determine the extent of the area within which the wreck lies; and to locate coin and artefacts more precisely within that area. This sounds a relatively simple task, even though, as has already been described, the sea-bed comprises a jumble of boulders overgrown with kelp. However, no large artefacts were discovered clear of the boulders; all were buried or lodged deep down in cracks and crevices. There was one exception – there is always one – and that was the cannon discovered in 1964, which is believed to have been found unburied. Here then is one of the biggest mysteries of the *Liefde*. Where are the remaining 39 cannon?

Various visual search methods were employed, and not surprisingly these methods varied according to the type of underwater terrain. Regrettably, the simple 'towed diver' search was of no value over the kelp, which effectively forms a blanket over the boulders. Further, the search is too fast to permit every crevice and crack to be explored. The type of search used and found to be reasonably effective is known as a sea-bed jackstay search, which operates as shown in Fig. 4.

(a) Two parallel lines of easily seen cordage (white nylon, or polypropylene) are laid out and firmly anchored at their ends – at right angles to any tidal stream.

(b) A swimline (length of light line with a small weight at each end) is stretched between jackstays.

(c) Divers, one each side, then search along the swimline and, on reaching the other end, move it in the search direction. If the terrain is smooth, this distance is governed by visibility; otherwise by the amount which can be searched without leaving a gap – about six feet on the *Liefde* site.

(d) The divers swim back in the opposite direction and on reaching the jackstay, move the swimline . . . and so on.

This method was not 100 per cent effective over the type of terrain found round the *Liefde*, as the jackstay and swimline were frequently

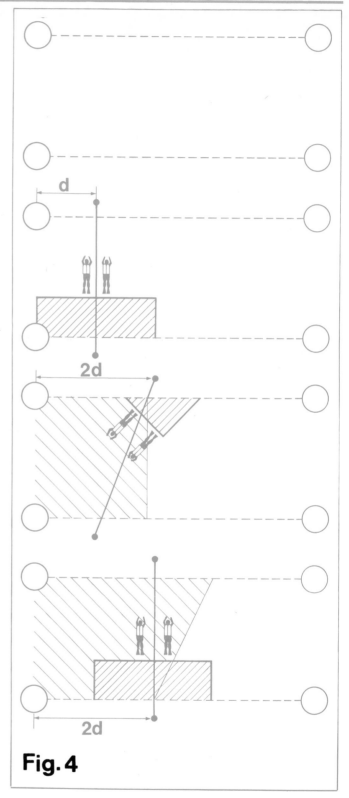

Fig. 4

Fig. 4. *The jackstay search method (described left) was used to survey the wreck site.*

well above the diver or obscured by boulders and kelp. Also, experience showed that it was necessary to straighten out the swimline after each move, as it often caught in the kelp or

Above. *Remains of a treasure chest recovered from the wreck of the **Liefde**. Suprisingly few coins were recovered from her cargo of silver.*

round a boulder. Unless this was done regularly, some areas were searched four or five times, and others not at all. It was also necessary to keep a record of where divers finished their search, and in which direction they were headed, otherwise the next pair could move the wrong end of the swimline and again gaps would be left.

Mention has already been made of the magnetometer, and indeed one was taken to the site on three of the five expeditions. Unfortunately the magnetic searches were not as successful as had been hoped for, the main reason being that they required the site to be clear of other work. And because a voluntary team of divers was being used, a lay-off of several days was difficult to justify. Further, a magnetometer search technique had to be evolved, and modified to suit the conditions at the site. This took time; one just cannot take an untried instrument, however simple – and magnetometers are not simple – and give it to a diver who has never seen it before, and obtain sensible results without considerable trial and error.

Survey work

It is in this sphere that commercial and marine archaeological interests conflict most. From the archaeological standpoint it is vital to map the area reasonably accurately before excavation is started, and to date the map as progress is made. It is only by doing this that work on the site can be effectively directed, and records compiled of sufficient accuracy to allow a proper evaluation of the positions where 'treasure' is most likely to be found. This of course takes time and conflicts with the commercial requirement to lift coin and artefacts, for subsequent sale, in order to make an expedition financially viable.

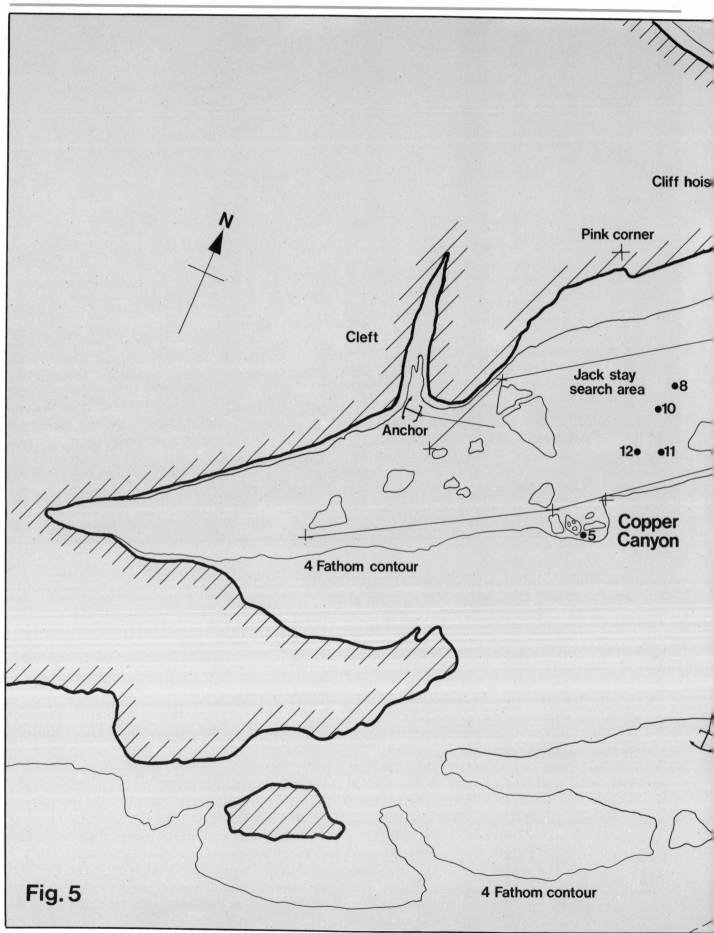

Cliff hois

Pink corner

Cleft

Anchor

Jack stay
search area

●8

●10

12● ●11

Copper
Canyon

●5

4 Fathom contour

Fig. 5

4 Fathom contour

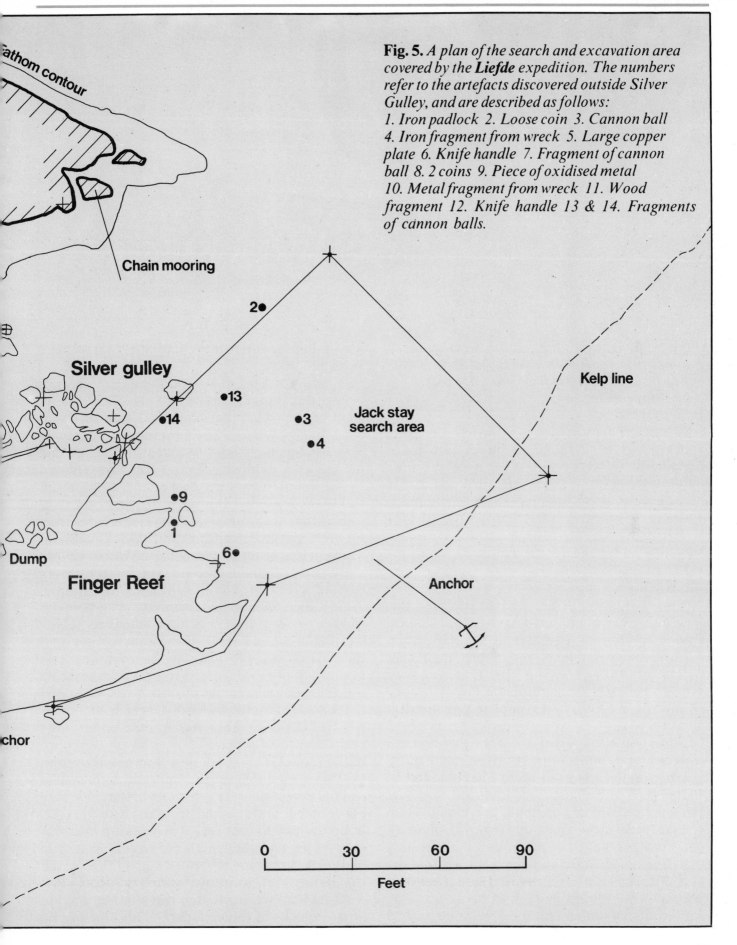

Fig. 5. *A plan of the search and excavation area covered by the **Liefde** expedition. The numbers refer to the artefacts discovered outside Silver Gulley, and are described as follows:*
1. Iron padlock 2. Loose coin 3. Cannon ball 4. Iron fragment from wreck 5. Large copper plate 6. Knife handle 7. Fragment of cannon ball 8. 2 coins 9. Piece of oxidised metal 10. Metal fragment from wreck 11. Wood fragment 12. Knife handle 13 & 14. Fragments of cannon balls.

Fathom contour

Chain mooring

Silver gulley

2●

●13

●14

●3

●4

Jack stay
search area

Kelp line

●9

1

6●

Dump

Finger Reef

Anchor

chor

0	30	60	90

Feet

Above. *Although very little gold or silver was recovered from the* **Liefde,** *objects like these horn knife handles add to our knowledge of life in 18th century Europe.*

As no wreckage such as timber or large artefacts had been found, a survey had to be carried out to show both a plan of the area round the wreck and a more detailed plan of the sea-bed where most material had been found.

Although some work was carried out in 1966 by Ian Morrison no further detailed surveys were made until the 1968 expedition.

Excavation

Various words might be used to describe this work; but 'excavation', used in its archaeological sense, is preferred. The aim of the excavation was to remove artefacts and debris in a controlled manner, leaving the true sea-bed revealed beneath. Because of the highly broken terrain, this aim was not completely realized at the wreck site.

Excavation was carried out in two main areas – Silver Gulley and Copper Canyon (see Fig. 5). In Silver Gulley, rocks of up to 250 cubic feet in volume had to be raised and dumped, together with smaller boulders, pebbles, gravel and sand. In 1965 little more than the removal of small rocks and pebbles took place, and in 1966 only rock fragments and boulders which could be manhandled were removed from the site. Explosives were used in 1966 to break up rock, and this also revealed that the area to be probed

was much greater than had originally been supposed.

It was not until 1967 that major clearance began, and it is interesting to see the development of the techniques employed – all of which were man-powered. First a service kit-bag, filled with fragments, was hauled clear of the site and the contents dumped. The kit-bag was replaced by a fisherman's wicker basket and a block and tackle used to haul the basket clear of the bottom. Finally, a metal pontoon some ten feet square was fitted with a chain block capable of lifting rocks of up to two tons weight in water.

By these methods several tons of rock were carried clear of Silver Gulley and dumped against the cliff some 20 feet away. The pontoon worked well, but it was very sensitive to the weather – the speed of lifting was so slow that the 'snatch' on the gear as the rock was just clearing the seabed proved too great in anything but the calmest weather.

1968 saw the advent of a larger boat (an ex RN 'H.L.D.' 52½ feet long), and the opportunity was taken to fit a petrol-driven winch starboard of the funnel. The purchase wire was led over an 'A' frame mounted on the transom. This system worked reasonably well once its limitations were appreciated, and it could be used in sea heights of up to three to four feet. The working load was only 5 cwt, and the length of the purchase wire had to be limited – too great a length increased the drum size and the winch stalled. The working load was increased threefold by the use of two blocks in the system, and still further by

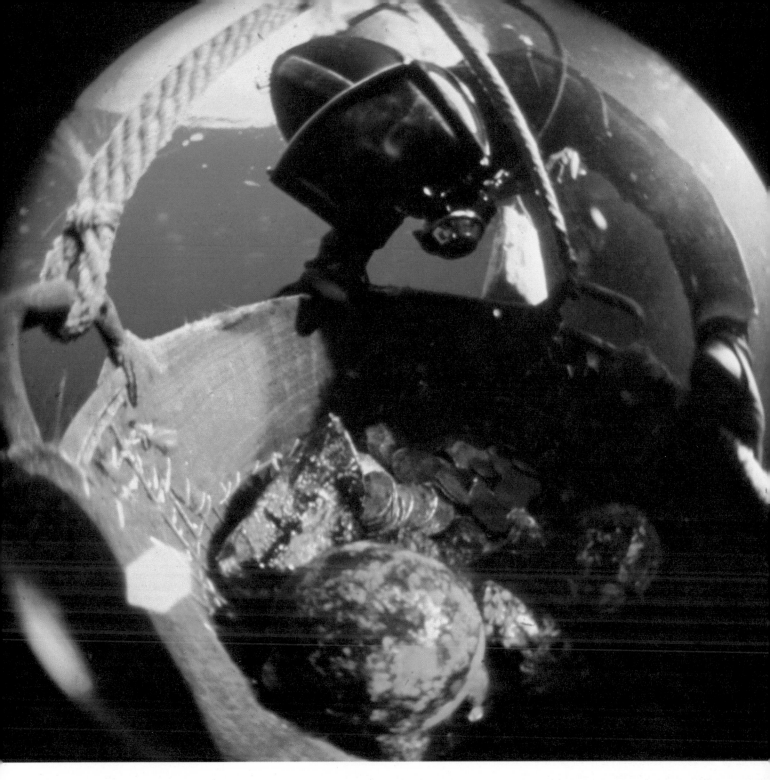

attaching up to three air lifting-bags to the loads. Each bag gave a lift of 300 lb.

The second area in which excavation took place was called Copper Canyon. This is an indentation midway along the north side of the reef, which contained a large jagged plate of copper wedged firmly between rocks. Having first been photographed in colour, the plate was removed by two divers using a pickaxe and brought to the surface with the aid of an air-bag.

The dumping of cleared material proved to be more complex than was first appreciated. In the

Above. *The fish-eye lens captures a diver clearing debris taken from the wreck site. Heavy rock-falls have covered much of the wreck.*

first three years, debris was dumped at the foot of the cliff north of Silver Gulley – in July 1968 it was dumped on the reef. As work progressed, it was appreciated that the dispersal of the wreck could be such that artefacts might be buried in both these areas. Thus, for the latter half of 1968, all debris was brought to the boat and dumped some 500 yards away.

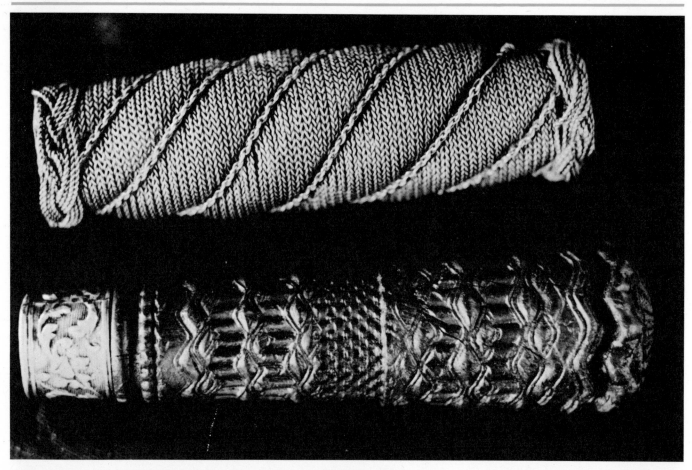

Through trial and error the most satisfactory excavation procedure was arrived at. The order of work was as follows:
(1) Map and photograph the area.
(2) Blast with minimum explosive.
(3) Map and photograph the result – to be used for diver briefing.
(4) Clear larger rocks by winch, smaller by loading into nets. Loads then suspended from the boat, and dumped 500 yards away.
(5) Larger artefacts revealed and photographed in situ before being lifted.

Artefacts and coins

Artefacts and coins were recovered in four different situations. First, in Silver Gulley they were buried in a hard black substance which has been described by an analyst of the London Institute of Archaeology as: 'a matrix composed largely of sulphides'. The matrix appeared to have been poured by some giant hand, and had found a level around and among the boulders of the gulley which slopes down from north to south. It appeared that there had been a minor, if not a major, cliff rock-fall since the formation of the matrix.

Second, in a lesser state of preservation, artefacts were found in the mixture of gravel, sand, and small pebbles which filled in between the boulders of the Gulley – generally below the matrix. What is possibly the ship's lead and several cannon balls lying in the gravel mixture were photographed as they were revealed by the airlift.

Third, other objects were found in the general area surrounding Silver Gulley. They were generally small, and all were in a bad state of preservation.

Over the years articles have been washed ashore. Coins have been discovered on the cliffs north of the site, particularly after a traditionally 'great' storm such as occurred in 1900. A cannon ball was also found on a beach a mile east of the site in 1968, and there is 'talk' of a gold bar having been found wedged in the rocks between tides, and never recovered . . .

So far the material recovered may be split into the following categories:

Multiple items	Single items
Coin	Cannon
Bar Shot	Copper Plate
Cannon Balls	Ship's Bell
Trading Goods	Seal
Ship's Fittings	Sounding Lead
Small fragments of:	Wooden Chest
Wood	
Pottery	
Glass	
Metal	
Canvas	
Breech Blocks	

In conclusion, it would appear that there are one or two mysteries surrounding the wreck of the *Liefde* and her missing cargo. Where, for example, are the cannon? Originally it was thought that the single cannon had been carried only as ballast, as it was badly worn and corroded. However, in 1968, during the course of a dive in the vicinity of the site of the *Kennermerlandt*, another cannon was found. It, too, was in a bad state, being so corroded at the muzzle end of the barrel that the bore was revealed. These were the only two cannons found from a reputedly heavily-armed ship.

It seems unlikely that the remaining cannon had simply corroded away or been battered to pieces by high seas. Besides, two of the *Liefde's* cannons were of bronze. Nor is it likely that the cannons were jettisoned before the sinking – reports indicate that the ship struck without any warning. Even if the upper deck guns had been ditched, the crew would not have risked opening the lower ports in order to get rid of the lower deck guns.

It appears that the bulk of the *Liefde's* valuable cargo was salvaged soon after the wreck. But this does not explain the absence of large quantities of less valuable artefacts such as china, tin or ship's utensils. Perhaps they lie buried under a landslide: certainly there are indications that such phenomena have occurred round the site.

Another, better equipped expedition intends revisiting the site and perhaps it may solve the mystery of the ship's missing cargo. No doubt some aspects of the mysterious wreck will be solved, but it seems likely that the rest of the *Liefde's* secrets have been lost forever.

Top left. *Remains of a sword hilt and a walking stick recovered in 1967.*
Bottom left. *Breech blocks from cannon. Only two of the* **Liefde's** *guns have been located.*

CARIBBEAN GOLD

Alexander McKee

If you live on a coast where the main ship traffic consists of dirty colliers, the only treasure you are likely to find will be 'black diamonds'. And although every wreck, even a sunken motor boat, has some value, if only for its fittings, it is a rare vessel that contains an entire cargo which may be properly described as 'treasure'. The great exception is that coastline bordering the Caribbean, from Bermuda and Florida in the north, to Cartagena and Porto Bello in the south; for this was the centre of the great two-ocean system of convoys known as the Plate Fleets, which for three centuries transported to Spain the rarest and richest products of the Indies.

And not of the Indies only, for on the Pacific side of the narrow land-bridge formed by the isthmus of Panama, were the sea routes from Peru and Manila. The loot of the Inca empire, and the products of trade with China via the Phillipines, were conveyed overland to Caribbean ports, for loading into Spanish ships which would eventually rendezvous at Havana. From here they would combine into one great convoy, escorted by a squadron of fighting galleons, for the homeward voyage past Florida and the Bahamas, with Bermuda their last landfall in the new world.

The wooden hulls held the richest cargoes of their age and for this reason they were well guarded. The capture of a Spanish convoy could be achieved only after a fleet action fought by a major European power. Many tried, few succeeded. As a matter of record, 93 per cent of the gold galleons and 91 per cent of the merchant ships and dispatch vessels made uneventful voyages, in spite of hurricanes, casual pirates and even enemy battle squadrons. It was a notable achievement of Spanish organisation and military skill.

A death-trap for shipping

But what of the losses? The seven per cent and the nine per cent? The greater part were concentrated in the Caribbean – for two reasons. It is a shallow sea of innumerable islands and coral reefs, poorly charted and with many unpredictable currents and tidal sets. Also, it is subject to hurricanes at certain times of the year, when much of it becomes in effect one enormous lee shore – a terrible ship trap no matter from which direction the wind blows. And in a hurricane the winds scream landwards at more than 75 m.p.h. often at more than 100 m.p.h., raising waves so high that nearby ships in a convoy are hidden from sight in the troughs. Sailing ships caught close to the shallows in such conditions are in deadly peril and almost powerless to avoid it; and although the Spaniards planned their sailings to avoid the hurricane season they were not always successful. More treasure fleets perished this way than from capture by the Dutch or British.

However, one factor which tended to take toll of the treasure ships also facilitated the salvage of part or all of the treasure – often by the Spaniards themselves. This was the fact that the wrecks occurred most often by stranding in the shallows, rather than by sinking in deep water far out at sea. The average depth range of wrecks in the area is around 30 feet; well within reach of a naked diver submerging merely by holding his breath. And except in the aftermath of a hurricane or off a sand or mud shore, the water is usually exceptionally clear. Objects on the sea-bed can be seen by the naked eye from a boat; it is not even always necessary to use a glass-bottomed bucket as a peephole.

Right. *Aided by sophisticated electronic equipment, American treasure hunters have found many Spanish Plate Fleet wrecks.*

Above. *Sir William Phips was the first to mount a full-scale treasure hunt in the Caribbean. Using native divers he recovered £1,500,000 worth of bullion from one wreck alone.*

If the area of the wreck was known – sometimes it was a big 'if' – then it was the owners of the treasure who mounted the first salvage operation. When the site became uneconomic for them to work, it was abandoned to the local 'wrackers', who swarmed in for the lesser pickings. But after a comparatively short time, what remained would be hard to see and virtually impossible to recover, because of the rapid growth of coral over the wreckage, and a phenomenon caused by the presence of iron in the wreck – the fusing of the sea-bed sediments around it into a hard 'concretion'. Before the invention of efficient diving apparatus, it required luck and a good deal of money, power and sheer organisation to secure a treasure which the Spaniards themselves had failed to recover.

Treasures of Silver Shoals

A notable example was the operation carried out by William Phips, a New England shipmaster and merchant, in 1687 on the wreck of *La Nuestra Senora de la Concepcion*, stranded on the Silver Shoals in 1641. Although a fairly recent sinking, much of the treasure was already out of reach. According to Phips, 'The greatest part of the treasure lay aft of the mainmast, which part of the ship was so overgrown with coral that it was never able to be cleared away'. His problem was not so much to pick up coins from the sea-bed, but to break off the encrusting coral and then smash the pieces on deck to reveal what was inside. Not always did he find what he hoped for, but on one occasion, from inside a single piece of coral, 'there was found 7,600 dollars, and these dollars were very bright and not damnified at all by the water'.

This was enormously hard work, in which Phips employed 300 native divers operating from 100 boats protected by two armed ships, the largest mounting 22 guns, against the intervention of pirates. His backing came from powerful Court Circles in England, and his equipment included large air reservoirs in the form of tubs six feet high and ten feet wide, which were lowered to within a few feet of the sea-bed. When the native skin-divers ran out of breath, they surfaced inside the tubs for a short rest, thus in theory saving the energy normally consumed in diving. The tubs were a kind of underwater base in which the air would gradually have become more and more toxic.

Below. *The recovery of this silver coin, dated 1732, was a clue to the location of a Spanish Plate Fleet lost in 1733.*
Right. *Hunting for coins along the tide-line.*

After three months work the divers were exhausted, but their recoveries totalled 170 tons of silver in coins and bars, as well as valuable silver dishes and plate and a certain amount of gold to a total value of about £1½ million sterling. Yet this was not the bulk of the treasure, which remained too deep under coral to be touched and is probably still there to this day, entombed in the heart of the reef.

In modern times many expeditions have sought the treasure of Silver Shoals, including Jacques-Yves Cousteau, the inventor of the aqualung, in his research ship *Calypso*. Led to a wreck by local information, as Phips had been before him, he too set his divers to work chipping coral for month after month. There were signs that other people had been at work, using explosives, before giving up the quest. But Cousteau carried on, raising cannon, anchors, ship fittings and pottery until he found an artefact with an actual date on it. The inscribed year was 1756, more than a century after the sinking of the great treasure ship. Cousteau promptly named his wreck the *Nuestra Senora de la Decepcion*, but at least got a book and a film out of his work on her.

Pieces of eight

Dating from scattered, coral-encrusted remains, let alone identifying the actual ships of which they were once a part, is not so easy as it may appear; but it helps to be knowledgeable about the ships and cargoes of the period. There is an insidious process which, if not resisted, may turn the most fevered treasure seeker into a part-time historian and antiquarian (rarely into an archaeologist, because of the lure of treasure, but this does happen, too). The affliction is more frequently found among the locals than among the visitors from overseas, but is nevertheless very real. Few men find treasure ships; those who do rarely find just one, they find many.

An instance to show how this unfair process works is the discovery, by Teddy Tucker, of the *San Antonio* sunk 20 years before the *Nuestra Senora de la Concepcion* on the reefs of Bermuda in 1621. He and his friends were scouring

Left. *Fast-growing coral soon covers objects on the sea-bed, and makes clear identification of wrecks extremely difficult. The diver must learn to evaluate unusual coral formations.*

the reefs from their boat, looking down through the water for any unnatural shapes or patterns which might be the only immediate clue to the presence of a wreck. This, of course, implies knowledge of the natural patterns. After some hours they located a 'probable', which turned out to be a wreck, but of the wrong type. There were traces of copper sheathing – an anti-ship-worm device introduced only in the late 18th century – together with fittings and artefacts which suggested a late 19th century ship. So they carried on along the reefs for a short while before seeing traces of another wreck. It took only one dive to 25 feet to convince Tucker that the remains had been there a very long time, while broken pottery fragments were quite sufficient for him to judge that the ship had been Spanish.

The question was: had anyone been there before him? There were some valuable objects about, including links from a gold chain, a pair of brass navigational dividers, jewellery, including an emerald, and an encrusted object which turned out to contain 43 silver 'pieces of eight', marked as coming from the famous Potosi mines in Peru. There was great excitement when Tucker found an eroded, but intact, wooden box buried in the sand and they had visions of a treasure chest. But when he pulled off one side of the box, a blue paste-like substance was revealed which clouded the water and stained his hands when he touched it. The 'treasure chest' was a case of indigo dye being shipped home to Spain. After a 346 year delay in its travels, the contents of the box were sent back to America, North, not South, and were used to paint a showcase in the Smithsonian Institute devoted to finds from the *San Antonio*.

She was indeed a treasure ship carrying more than 60,000 Crowns worth of gold and silver, but the British governor of Bermuda, Nathanial Butler, had got most of it, together with ten cannon, six swivel guns and four anchors. The single cannon he left on the bottom to mark the wreck site had been bored off-centre and so was probably thought not worth the salvage effort. Many of the smaller items had immediately been lifted by a swarm of local seamen; but much of what they had ignored was now of historic interest. There were cowrie shells, a form of primitive currency, in their thousands, and these must first have been carried across the Pacific in the Manila galleons before being mule-hauled overland to be loaded in the *San Antonio*, in 1621. There were mother-of-pearl shells, and these probably came from the Isle of Margarita in the Caribbean, where the Spaniards maintained a base for controlling the pearl divers. There was an olive jar, surprisingly intact, as evidence of the most popular form of Spanish 'containerisation'; logs of the rare hardwood *Lignum vitae,* in demand at that time for making the blocks which control a ship's rigging; and another exotic American product – the twisted leaves of tobacco.

The wealth of the Indies

The *San Antonio* was not the first treasure ship which Tucker had found. In 1951 he discovered a wreck which he called the *'Old Spaniard'.* From a boat he saw odd patterns lying on the sea-bed below him; they proved to be encrusted cannon which he raised and sold to Bermuda's Monuments Trust. Four years of Sunday diving passed before he decided to take another look at the site, and this time he was more experienced; used to spending hour after hour on the bottom, fanning the sand with his hands or a piece of board; stripping the sea-bed evenly, layer by layer. The method now turned up several silver coins and a 2 ounce gold cube within two hours. The discovery made secrecy vital. Within six days the find had been multiplied many times. Some of the gold bars were inscribed 'Pinto', which identified their origin as the Pinto river in New Granada. Those of the silver coins which were lying loose looked like blobs of tar speckled with sand, so bad was the corrosion; William Phips would have said they were 'damnified'. The only coins to retain most of their original silver content were those which had been in contact with iron on the sea-bed.

Gold, however, is unaffected by the chemical action of seawater and, on the seventh day of digging, Tucker saw a flash of gold in the swirling cloud of murk he was raising with an experimental water-jet. Grasping the object before it could vanish, he found himself looking at a gold cross studied with seven brilliant green

Top right. *Bar shot, designed to bring down the rigging of a sailing ship, is displayed next to a model of a cannon of the same period.*
Right. *Robert Marx, a pioneer underwater treasure hunter and archaeologist, arranges a collection of artefacts from a Spanish wreck.*

Left. *Spanish colonists in the New World robbed the natives of their great wealth: in return they gave them religion.*
Above. *Identifying Caribbean wrecks is confusing: their cargo was international and often included such items as this English watch.*

stones. A year later the British Museum confirmed what Tucker suspected, that they were not coloured glass but emeralds. This cross, together with a collection of gold buttons set with pearls found near it, could have belonged to a dignitary of the Church, perhaps a bishop of the late 16th century. It was a very old wreck indeed, and the cross, valued at £16,000 was then the most valuable single object ever to have been recovered from the sea. It is now displayed, together with other finds from the wreck, at the town hall in Hamilton, the capital of Bermuda.

However, it was possible that the ship had been carrying a much greater treasure which had already been salvaged, as was the case with another wreck of similar date and also found by Tucker. This one was marked by its ballast

stones lying on the coral. By removing the sand nearby with an underwater suction pump known as an airlift, part of the bottom timbers of the hull were exposed to view. This section measured 46 feet by 28 feet, and although the structure had been strongly and solidly built, it had been broken like a matchstick by the fierce pounding of the hull on the reef. Only a few intact artefacts remained and these were mostly of brass, lead and wrought-iron; the few silver coins left were utterly corroded.

The missing cargo could have been of gold and silver, and possibly mercury, for it was in about 1555 that the Spaniards introduced a separation process, requiring mercury, which made it profitable to work the many gold and silver deposits of the Indies. At first they had to import Hungarian mercury from Europe, but later discovered a mine in Peru. Spanish ships outward bound for the New World carried little that would nowadays be called treasure (and that applies also to many of the return cargoes, such as hides, dyes, timber and silk), but the single important exception is mercury, which is nowadays so costly that it ranks with the precious metals.

But it is also true that objects which were slightly out of the ordinary, such as Aztec or Inca or Indian 'souvenirs' being brought home by Spanish seamen, are now of great historic and anthropological value, as are items of equipment, such as navigational instruments. When Harry Cox, of Bermuda, following another ballast-stone clue, discovered a Spanish or Portuguese wreck of around 1580, the pearls and the many gold objects – including a 15 feet double link chain – took second place in interest to a mariner's astrolabe, of which there were then only 23 examples known in the world.

A cache of pirate guns

Before making their dangerous last landfall at Bermuda, the treasure fleets from Havana had first to traverse the Straits of Florida, with its hazards of islands and reefs, and further north the lee shore beaches of the mainland. Opposite was the long island chain of the Bahamas, not under Spanish control, where fast, heavily-manned pirate craft waited for the unfortunate straggler. There is always the slow ship and the vessel that has suffered some mishap to her rigging from bad weather.

But pirates were not immune from the perils

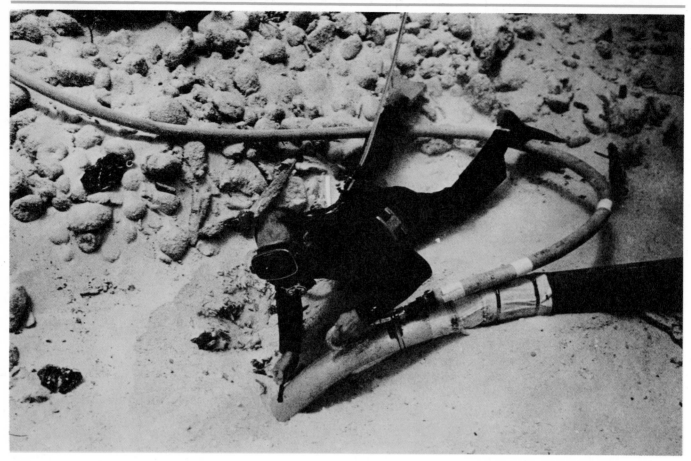

of the sea, and in 1966 Robert Wilkie and two other American spear-fishermen, hunting in 25 feet of clear water off Highborn Key, found a strange-looking wreck site which may be that of a very early privateer – possibly mid-16th century. The ballast-stones, guns and iron fittings were so well camouflaged by growth that they seemed part of the reef. There were no personal belongings or weapons left, so it seemed that the crew had time to escape. The ship's armament remained, however, and these guns were not 'cannon' at all in the technical sense. They were wrought-iron breech-loaders of early design, with detachable gunpowder chambers. Two were large, long and narrow long-range guns; either serpentines or slings. There were about a dozen smaller pieces, most of which were obviously swivel-guns, although it would be hard to give a correct name to them. Perhaps they were of the type known as a 'base'.

The number of such guns in existence is not great and the way in which they developed, the meaning of their names even, is not clear; so although not 'treasure' in the generally accepted sense, it would be difficult to put a price on them. On the other hand, as so many modern

Above. *Modern wreck-hunting equipment includes a powerful suction pump, capable of dredging mud and debris from a wreck site.*

treasure seekers have found to their dismay, iron guns, if left untreated, simply fall to pieces: their valuable souvenirs simply disintegrate in front of their eyes in the course of a few years. This is true of most materials found in wrecks and the answer can be expensive; conservation treatment in a special laboratory costing, in the case of a large gun, many hundreds of pounds.

Victims of the hurricanes

At least three Spanish Pate Fleets were almost totally lost in hurricanes. Some went down in deep water, but more were driven ashore. The earliest disaster was in 1553, near Padre Island, on what is now the coast of Texas. Hardly any of the thousands of men involved survived the twin perils of the hurricane waves at sea and the savage Indians on the shore; so it is unlikely that much, if any salvage, was undertaken at the time. One of these ships is reported to have been found, and to have yielded a certain amount of treasure and also some very old breech-loading

guns and a crossbow. Others are rumoured to have been located by a rich syndicate equipped with a wide variety of the latest wreck-finding equipment, including magnetometers. It is alleged that the syndicate 'excavated' the sites with explosives, leaving only great, ship-shaped craters remaining to show where these wrecks – which were of great historical value – once lay.

The last great disaster caused by bad weather was in 1733, when a hurricane hit the fleet two days out from Havana, in the vicinity of the Florida Keys. More than 20 ships were lost and only half the men survived. What is probably the remains of the flagship *Rui* was one of the first galleon discoveries of recent times. She was found in 1949 by a helmet-diver from Florida, Arthur McKee, in about 30 feet of water. The armament of heavy, cast-iron muzzle-loading guns was still there, as well as small-arms such as muskets and pistols. None of the bars of silver with which this ship was known to be loaded have been found, although the recoveries by McKee included silver and gold coins and some gold jewellery. A few very rare pillar dollars of 1732 were uncovered, and also an intriguing silver statue of a flamenco dancer, wearing a dress still seen today in Andalusia.

In the 1960s, several more wrecks believed to be from the 1733 fleet were located off Florida – at Uslamadora and Tavernier. The first produced some silver, the second the first human skull to be reported found in such a wreck; although whether the victim was a crew member, or one of the divers who so effectively sought the treasure for the Spaniards, is not known. For years after the ships were wrecked, part of the hulls might have shown clear of the surface of the crystal-clear water, making location, identification and salvage a very much easier matter than it is in modern times, when all the exposed woodwork has been gone for centuries and the one thing the remains do not resemble is a Spanish treasure ship.

Below. *A corroded sword hilt and a skull, recovered from the wreck of a Spanish treasure ship sunk in the great hurricane of 1733, give a clue to the dangers and hardships which the Spanish adventurers endured in their quest to capture the riches of the New World.*

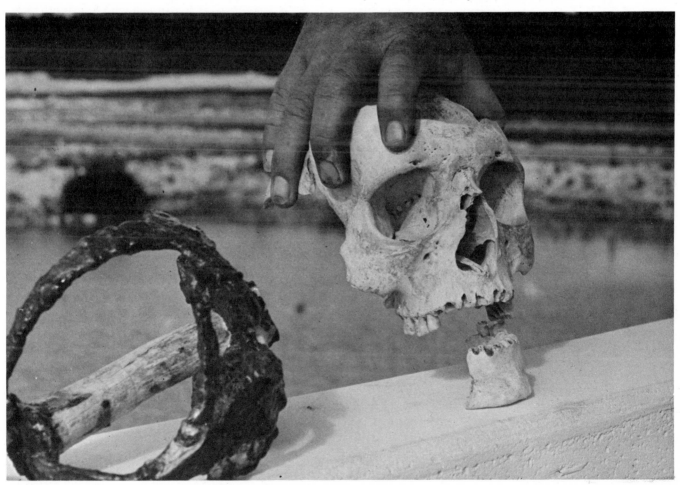

Blurred voices from the past

Even with expert museum assistance it is not always easy to state the nationality of the vessel, let alone its date or name. Coins in small quantities are not a good clue, anymore than they would be in the wreck of a modern airliner; and the ship remains on the reefs represent essentially international vehicles which have met with a nasty accident. A case in point was the exploration of a wreck on Looe Key, in which an American family, Barney and Jane Crile and their children, were the moving spirits. They carried out a holiday dig on a cannon site shown them by a friend and soon turned up some corroded coins. Two were Spanish, but others were French, and others again were Scandinavian. The wreck finally turned out to be British, the 44 gun frigate H.M.S. *Looe* which, sunk in 1744, gave her name to the reef which had destroyed her.

Another story of twists and turns in the evidence, with a similar surprise ending, was unravelled by Bob Marx and Clay Blair when they set out to probe a cannon site at Cozumel, off the coast of Yucatan. Blair's first impression was that there was no wreck there, so thoroughly were the remains concreted and covered by coral. After much coral had been cracked open and a hoard of artefacts removed, they decided that their Spanish galleon on the reef of Matanceros must be an unknown British frigate, which they christened H.M.S. *Woolworth* because of the great variety of objects she had carried! Only after several seasons work did it become clear that the vessel really was Spanish, but bound from Spain to the New World with a cargo of European goods destined for the colonists. And that the name Matanceros, given to the nearest landmark, did not mean 'Slaughter Point' as they had thought, but was in fact derived from the popular name for the ship, *Matanzero* (her real name was *Nuestra Senora de los Milagros*), probably because she had been built at Matanzas in Cuba. Once again the clue to identity had been there all the time in a local place-name, for ship disasters tend to be remembered.

Later, memories fade and the real clues lie hidden in old documents, so that many shipwrecks are really found on land, long before the searcher actually goes out to find them. This was true of the lost Plate Fleet of 1715, one of the richest, lost firstly in a hurricane and then by the historians who indicated two sites for the disaster some 200 miles apart, neither of them the right one. It was a housebuilder, Kip Wagner, of Sebastian, Florida, who over a period of many years accurately observed his local beaches, thoughtfully pondered over what happened to them during gales, carried out the appropriate research in archives and, convinced of the magnitude of his potential find, built up the right sort of team, obtained legal cover, and set out to look for – not a treasure ship – but a treasure fleet. There had been ten ships lost in one night off his local beaches and he found eight of them.

The greatest prize of all

His recoveries made all others seem, for the first time, exactly what they were – the inconsiderable trifles overlooked by salvage divers over the centuries. Phips had been the only really successful known operator, but then the Silver Shoals wreck was still of recent occurrence in his time. Not that the Spaniards had failed to dive for the treasures of the 1715 Plate Fleet; far from it. Wagner's research turned on this point, for he reasoned that if the fleet had indeed been wrecked off Sebastian, then the Spaniards must have established a salvage base. So he looked first for that, on land, and found it with the aid of an old mine detector.

The Spaniards, led to the sites by survivors, mounted a major salvage operation six months later, in which they employed 280 native divers and carried on work for nearly four years. Wagner's guess is that they recovered the more easily accessible items, amounting to perhaps less than half the treasure, and his diggings at the Spanish camp site showed that a pirate raiding party, probably English, had hijacked some of it. The local 'wrackers' of the Caribbean, who made a speciality out of 'fishing' treasure wrecks when the piracy business was bad, probably made their hauls, too; but many of the sites were not easy for native divers to

Top right. *This small glass triangle, etched with a cross, was recovered from the wreck of the **Nuestra Senora de Aviso**, sunk in 1733. It was the crucifix at the end of a rosary.*
Right. *Restored to its former glory, a gun-deck of the Swedish ship, the **Wasa**, salvaged from Stockholm harbour, shows how marine archaeology can benefit the historian.*

Above. *It took over a year of underwater searching to find the component pieces of this rare Aztec pottery bowl.*

work on the unaided capacity of their lungs. Most of these galleons had stranded on a sloping beach, not sunk at the foot of coral reefs, and they had been battered to pieces in the raging surf by waves which survivors described as being 50 feet high. Sand in the shallows is extremely mobile on open beach profiles, and the broken structures would rapidly have covered. Indeed, Wagner's main problem was not to crack coral, but to move tons and tons of sand before the next blow put it all back again. And because of these conditions, underwater visibility was usually poor to downright awful, and the diving boats were often subject to vicious wave and swell action.

Wagner had to take the rough with the smooth. If the sites had provided perfect diving there would have been no real treasure, for the Spaniards would have got it all centuries before him. The proof that they had not was to be provided during years of work. Silver and gold coins were found lying loose under the sand, as they had been on other sites, but the divers also found solid stacks of silver coins fused together in the shape of their original wood or canvas containers. That was cargo treasure, not a doubt of it. And they found, on one wreck when the sand layer was blasted away, not just a rare gold coin or two, but a carpet of gold, from which they recovered in a single day 1,033 gleaming golden coins. This was cargo in bulk, not the contents of the captain's pockets.

And they got some of the senior officers' belongings, too, just as makeweight. The most spectacular was a long golden chain with a gold whistle on one end – the traditional insignia of a European Admiral, equivalent to a Field Marshal's baton. In 1967 it sold for £17,857. But the most amazing recoveries were all items of stacked cargo, including 28 undamaged examples of delicate K'ang Hsi pottery which had survived the 4,000 mile journey from China and the shipwreck in a hurricane – some of the packing material which had saved it still remained. There was also the rarest item ever to come from a Spanish treasure ship – an actual treasure chest! About 3 feet long by a foot wide and a foot deep, the blackened wooden box was

crammed with the 3,000 silver pieces-of-eight which had been stacked inside it 250 years before. Wagner and his associates opened a museum to display this and other finds which they did not intend to sell. The total value of their recoveries has been estimated at around $3,000,000.

But even this is small beer compared to the value of a single galleon which held no treasure at all – the largely intact Swedish *Wasa*, raised from the bottom of Stockholm Harbour for her historical interest alone, and now in process of restoration for permanent museum display at an estimated cost of £3,000,000. That really is big business and it is increasingly the business of the future.

Recreating the past

Until recently, the dice were loaded against the divers who wanted to excavate Plate Fleet wrecks carefully and methodically in order to obtain maximum information about them, and not merely items of 'treasure'. The Caribbean scene was that of wholesale pirating of treasure wrecks by private groups in association with corrupt State officials. To this end they employed considerable resources, including spotter aircraft. Anyone seriously excavating had to disguise his boat with fishing rods, children and bathing beauties. Airlifts, which send up tell-tale bubbles and sediment, could not be used; so dredges, which lie flat on the bottom while they pump or suck water, had to be the excavation tools.

Even with these handicaps, good results have been achieved. Carl M. Frederick of Miami, who began excavating treasure wrecks because that was what he had in his local waters, soon discovered that little real treasure remained but that sometimes a surprising amount of hull had survived – particularly when the wreck lay between reefs in a semi-protected area and the structure had broken at the keel. Starting with merely an exposed heap of ballast-stones or cannon, he has dug to 5 feet and exposed the whole side of a galleon for measuring and recording. From evidence obtained from one early Spanish wreck, he was able to show that the old breech-loading guns and the mortars which fired bomb-shells were concentrated aft, unlike the muzzle-loading stone-throwers–on the main gun-decks; and that the Indian pottery so often found in such wrecks was not cargo at all,

Above. *Every diver hopes for that 'once-in-a-lifetime' find. For Carl Frederick, this priceless K'ang Hsi cup came as close as anything to fulfilling his dreams.*

but crew souvenirs destined for the family mantelpiece in Spain. And these results were obtained from wrecks so exposed that a modern hurricane can lift and even move them some distance. The discovery of this fact was important, because it indicated the potential of those wrecks which sank on very soft sea-beds in deeper water, beyond the real reach of hurricane waves.

The early Spanish discoverers of the Indies lost a number of ships, and if only one sank in a position favourable for its preservation, that would be a find beyond price. Imagine a museum which could put on display not just encrusted anchors, corroded cannon and collections of familiar coins, but an actual ship of Columbus's fleet with much of its original contents in place. Or even a real treasure galleon with hull almost intact. These would be prizes well worth the virtual suppression of casual treasure hunting.

BRITAIN'S ARCHAEOLOGICAL TREASURES

Shiela Liebmann

The attraction of buried treasure has always been with us and has often been distorted by emotionalism. Modern archaeology seeks to strike a balance between imagination and a strictly scientific attitude. The excitability of even such reports as Howard Carter's from the Valley of the Kings on the Upper Nile when he found Tutankhamen's tomb – let alone Rider Haggard's from Zimbabwe – would not be thought faultless today. Yet inevitably the term 'buried treasure' seems to arouse a deeply romantic response in most people.

Below. *Beautifully worked treasures from Sutton Hoo revealed a hitherto unknown high culture.*
Right. *The vizored helmet found at Sutton Hoo sheds a unique light on the mysterious warring culture of the Dark Ages.*

Professor Stuart Piggott once remarked that archaeology is 'the science of rubbish'. And it is true that, to the archaeologist, any object from the past has value, whereas, till he learns better, the layman may remain unmoved by the mute messages conveyed by some dusty scrap of debris. But occasionally a discovery is made which captures the excitement and imagination of a whole nation. Such a spectacular discovery was that of the Saxon burial ship at Sutton Hoo.

On a crest between two coombes, near Woodbridge in Suffolk, above the tidal estuary of the River Deben, in a round barrow (one of 15), the discovery took place in 1939 of the grave goods of a Saxon king. They were contained in a clinker-built open rowing boat, 80 feet to 89 feet long, which was buried with its stern to the west. They surpassed anything previously even speculated about the Dark Ages. Gold abounded, most exquisitely ornamented with garnets and lapis lazuli. Among the treasures found were: 'Splendid barbaric jewels set with garnets and filigree ... jewelled sword-hilt ... vizored helmet ... hanging-bowls ... silver from Byzantium ... shield with boss decorated in gilded bronze set with garnets ... king's sword ... six-stringed harp in beaver-skin bag ... purse-clasp ... belt-buckle ... strap-distributor ... shoulder-clasps ... Scandinavian military heirlooms ... giant whetstone or sceptre ... golden harness ... solid gold equipment ...'

The Sutton Hoo discovery has an unique legal history. The quality and quantity of it caused immediate litigation which brought it into the limelight. It was eventually declared to be, not Treasure Trove, and therefore the property of the Crown, but the property of Mrs May Pretty, the owner of the site. In a fine gesture commensurate with the spirit of the ship itself, Mrs Pretty forthwith presented the discovery to the nation.

A vision of the Dark Ages

Bring me ancient silver, precious
Jewels, shining armour and gems ...
sang the warrior, Beowulf, during that gap in our knowledge aptly called the Dark Ages, which stretches between the spread of Christianity and the fade-out of paganism.

In the context of the discovery at Sutton Hoo, the epic saga of Beowulf took on a new dimension. Now its stirring lines were not only beautiful, they also made sense. The poet sang

Left. *Although the timbers of the Sutton Hoo burial ship have rotted away through the ages, archaeologists have been able to piece together the design of the ship down to its last detail.*
Above. *The sophistication of early British art is revealed in this gold buckle found at Sutton Hoo. Coiled and intertwining forms are a feature of Celtic and Viking art, and appear in the elaborate lettering of Medieval manuscripts.*

of real things, real customs, of which real evidence was now apparent. As a result, our knowledge of the lost period following the departure of the Romans has been immensely extended. Here is one example:

Above their heads glittered boar-crests of tempered gold

Keeping watch over the Geats . . .

These lines, like many in the epic *Beowulf,* were never considered as anything but romantic fantasy; but now, with the discovery of a warrior-king's helmet at Sutton Hoo, we can compare the real thing with that poetic description.

The great vizored helmet is one of the outstanding pieces in the Sutton Hoo collection which, incidentally, is on permanent display in the Edward VII Gallery at the British Museum. The wings of a kind of flying dragon form the eyebrows on the mask; its fanned-out tail, the intimidating moustache. The terminals of the crest plunge downwards towards this as if to meet an attack. A mightly battle is in progress, above the brow of a warrior. The 'boar-crests' of *Beowulf* are vindicated.

The circumstances of the Sutton Hoo discovery were as fantastic as the treasures them-

selves. The outbreak of World War II occurred almost simultaneously with the finding. The site had to be opened, examined, recorded and filled in again with bracken and sand at top speed, to make way for tank manoeuvres and to avoid the threat of German bombing and invasion.

The accuracy and thoroughness of that first excavation is all the more remarkable when we realise how impromptu it had to be. In 1939, no one in Britain had ever excavated a burial deposit remotely approaching, in importance or complexity, the burial ship; and no one had ever, apart from the recovery of prehistoric dug-out canoes from river mud, excavated a ship; especially one whose timbers had wholly disappeared. While the treasure itself was tangible, the ship, unlike the Viking ship found at Oseberg, in Norway, of which the timbers were wonderfully preserved, had totally disintegrated. It was a sort of ghost; a non-entity, except for its shadowy outline in the sand. Nevertheless, it was measured, drawn, understood, rebuilt down to its last clench-nail, scarf-bolt and rove.

Below. *This purse lid from Sutton Hoo bears a 'Daniel in the Lion's Den' motif.*

After the war ended, between 1965 and 1968 further excavations were undertaken by the Ministry of Works. Paul Ashbee, now of Norwich University, headed these, assisted by his wife. For a brief time I assisted this dedicated team of diggers, and have held in my palm one of the jewels, just after its rescue from over thirteen centuries of entombment – a memorable moment . . .

Tribute to a warrior-king

The date of the burial has recently been declared by Dr. J.P.C. Kent, on evidence newly acquired from Merovingian coins found in the ship. to be, not between 650 and 670 A.D. as was first assumed, but between 625 and 630 A.D. at the latest.

It has been proved that the ship was hauled, bows foremost, on rollers, in from the sea. The shoreline of the bay lay then at a distance of

Left. *This stag is thought to have been an emblem of the warrior-king commemorated at Sutton Hoo, and appears on his battle standard.*
Below. *Everything that the warrior-king was likely to need in the afterlife was buried in the ship – including domestic utensils.*

about 600 feet from the burial spot, though now it is half a mile away. The ship was then lowered into the trench prepared for it and ceremoniously covered, to the accompaniment of songs, harps and feasting. We may legitimately picture the huge iron cauldrons, emptied again and again of food; the auroch drinking horns, constantly replenished with wine; mourning voices, music, in the light of stars and fires. with sea winds blowing in from faraway Uppsala.

No traces of a body were found. The ship was supposed to be a cenotaph. Some recent tests, however, suggest the possibility that a body was, after all, contained in it. The dead man commemorated by the ritual may have been the Saxon King Raedwald. It is significant that Sutton Hoo lies only four miles from the ancient palace of the East Saxon monarchy at Rendlesham. Whatever or whoever he may have been. his accoutrements and possessions constitute the most magnificent collection of Anglo-Saxon funerary regalia ever found – 'the finest Dark Age jewellery of its class in Europe'.

Now the site is empty. Nothing remains but brooding stillness, broken only by the crying gulls and the sigh of the wind.

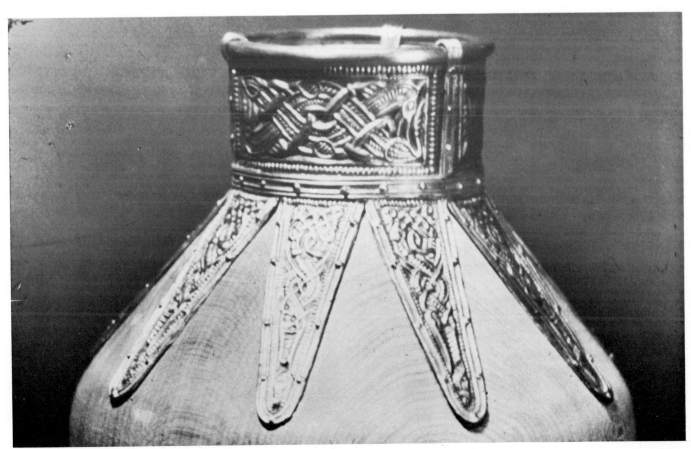

The palace at Fishbourne

Earlier in time than Sutton Hoo, the Roman remains at Fishbourne, in Sussex, also exert an extraordinary fascination. They date from the Roman invasion of Great Britain in 43 A.D. to about the end of the third century. Here we have no array of jewels; only an unparalleled perspective into the past; a panorama of human development, disaster and decay.

The Palace at Fishbourne is the largest domestic Roman complex ever discovered in Britain. It will be interesting presently to compare it with Lullingstone – the largest known Roman villa in Britain – which, though large, was not the home of a ruler.

It was in 1960 that the clues to the existence of the Palace were followed up, although indications of its existence had been discovered in 1805. In 1960, a workman cutting a watermain trench drew the engineer's attention to some odd-looking rubble. The engineer duly reported the matter to the local archaeological authorities. A series of excavations were subsequently sponsored by the Chichester Civic Society. They can never be finalised, for modern houses cover a lot of the vital area, which is also bisected by a modern main road, the A27. The extent of the complex is a barrier too – in that flat part of Sussex it seems to stretch as far as the eye can see.

The simplest way to assess the history of the site is to examine the various levels at which archaeological evidence has been found – each level indicating a different period in the history of the site. In this way a fascinating story builds up, reflecting not only the story of the palace itself, but also the fortunes of the Roman occupation of Britain.

Rising through the vertical section from its lowest stratum – 43 or 44 A.D. – we observe the changes as they happen. Originally, two Claudian buildings were constructed near a harbour, doubtless as military granaries and stores. They were built on piles, to protect their contents from rats and the damp rising from the marshy Sussex flatlands. One was positioned to the east of a stream which ran into a creek forming the northern end of Chichester Inlet, and between two new roads running east-west.

Right. *Nearly 2,000 years after it was buried, this Roman mosaic at Fishbourne, depicting a sea-leopard, is now restored to its former glory.*

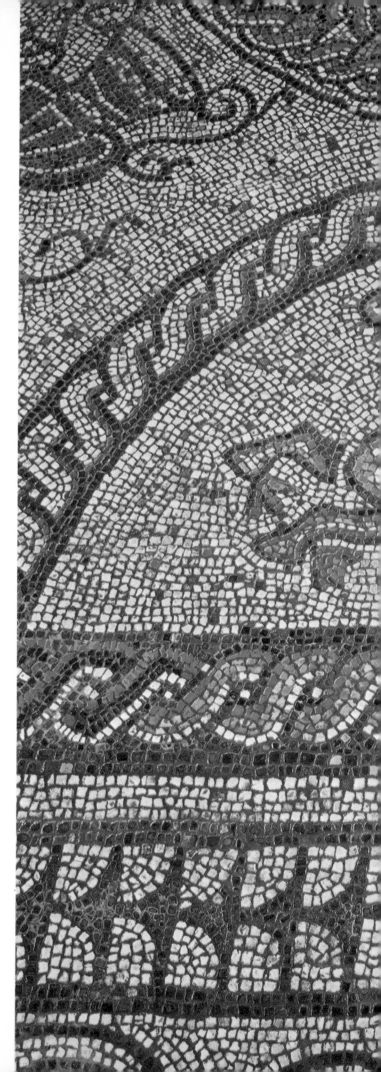

The other stood north of the northern road.

Examining the lowest stratum, we find evidence of two fords. The upper ford was eventually supplemented by a masonry foot-bridge, but retained for the use of transport and cattle, while the lower disappeared in the cause of better drainage. The harbour could take both deep-water and shallow-craft shipping. Though the land beyond was wild, it was the territory of the Atrebates, a tribe friendly to Rome. Fish-bourne in 43 A.D. offered inviting anchorage and an ideal position for a supply base.

Prosperity and splendour

Exciting developments follow, as we rise through the levels. Fishbourne, we see, pros-pered. After 30 years or so of specialised mili-tary usefulness, civilian buildings were inaugurated. About 75 A.D., a complete overhaul took place. The old military structures were replaced by an ambitious residence which must have had huge wealth expended on it, for its construction required magnificent materials and first-class craftsmen.

This was to be a very grand establishment indeed. The influence of the metalworkers and the masons, the painters, sculptors, mosaicists and gardeners were everywhere visible to the trained eye. Marble, from Carrara in Italy, from Turkey and from other sources in Medi-terranean lands, along with other varieties of beautiful ornamental stone, were freely import-ed and lavishly employed. Paintings, panelling, fine timber, stucco, mosaic floors abounded in the new rooms. These sumptuous transforma-tions continued enthusiastically until, some time between 110 and 270 A.D., it seems that someone in control had second thoughts, or received some mysterious edict that the style of the domicile was to be altered.

Some of the planned improvements were abandoned in mid-work – only to make way for a project still more grandiose. Fishbourne sud-denly assumed the aspect not merely of a rich man's splendid home, but of the regal palace of a ruler. What caused this metamorphosis? Why did Fishbourne suddenly turn into an imperial residence, unmatched anywhere else outside the confines of Rome?

There is no proof of what happened, but a plausible theory is that the site may have always belonged to the family of a native British king, Cogidubmus. Cogidubmus was what we should call a collaborator. He feathered his nest in no uncertain fashion by co-operation with Rome; but he seems to have been a great personality in his own right. He was awarded honours unequalled by any other member of his conquered race; they are recorded on a plaque no further away from Fishbourne than Chichester. He was given the right to sit on the Roman Senate; an unheard-of accolade for a non-Roman.

The soaring fortunes of Fishbourne, so ap-parent in the excavations, could well be explained by the rise of this British king to the status of a puppet-king under Roman rule. If this were so, Rome would spare no expense to buttress the power, extent and splendour of the office of the Emperor's representative in the Province.

One thing we can be sure of. During the years of Vespasion's success after the death of Nero, a tremendous edifice, richly appointed, and set in wide formal gardens, went up at Fishbourne. It continued to be maintained, modified, beau-tified and enlarged, apparently continuously, as if money was no object. But it was never finished.

So far, there had been movement and improvement all the way – from the erection of the first simple and comparatively rough mili-tary base close to the harbour, to the stately plan of apartments, with their mosaics, colonnades, altars, paintings, baths, and scented gardens sloping to the sea. Then, suddenly, everything was catastrophically destroyed in a great fire. From its Claudian debut to its Flavian finale, all ended at Fishbourne in a winding-sheet of flame.

Whether the fire was caused by carelessness or whether the Palace was raided by pirates, we cannot tell. We can stare at the remains of scorched lintels and rafters, melted roof lead, glass window-panes twisted by intense heat: but we cannot quite understand.

Shadows flow over the scene now. Perhaps, with the decision of Rome not to continue colonisation but to pull out of the Province in the cold northern seas, her ageing British *legatus augusti* lost heart and ambition. Whatever the cause, the entire site was abandoned. Its

Right. *The mute faces of Vespasian (left) and Nero (right) stare out from these Roman coins found at Fishbourne.*

Right. *A bishop, one of the fine medieval chessmen found on Lewis in 1831, stares blindly out from his throne.*
Far right. *The design of chess pieces has changed little in 1,000 years: this fine ivory knight has his counterpart in every modern chess set.*

deterioration after it had been stripped of reusable relics and materials can be clearly read in the evidence contained in the next levels – dated 270 and 400 A.D. Mists from the marshes gathered over it; gradually, as Rome declined, the earth buried it; the ploughs of the Middle Ages broke it, year by year; and the 20th century irrevocably sealed some of it under bricks and macadam and concrete.

It is surely all the more marvellous, that now, thanks to the trouble one man took to clamber down from his cumbersome excavator, the close green leaves of the box tree again edge the wide Flavian garden pathways – now restored with the ruins. Once again the rose and the lily, with rosemary and rue, fill the Sussex air with their perfume, as – no doubt in that same spot – they used to do, at Fishbourne, 15 centuries ago.

The Lewis hoard

Not all treasure is vast. One of the most modest, yet most interesting and deservedly famous discoveries of buried treasure in Britain – known as the Lewis Hoard – was made by a crofter at

Lough Resort in the Outer Hebrides in 1831.

This man was out working near some sandbanks. He had found them quite changed in shape, by a recent storm. I have seen a similar phenomenon myself, off the Suffolk coast, and it is very disturbing. The sensation of surprise and unfamiliarity is heightened by the hush in the atmosphere which follows a storm – when a gale capable of shifting tons of sand has at last blown itself out.

The crofter is often described as having been 'simple'. My sympathies are with him, however, for no one in the Outer Hebrides in 1831 can be expected to have been particularly sophisticated. However, he must certainly have been conditioned beforehand, subconsciously, by the weather and the wild scene. A nervous reaction was only natural.

First, having sustained the slight shock of finding himself in what seemed an unfamilia landscape, and looking, in consequence, witl more attention than usual at the dunes, he noticed some stonework in the sand which he had not seen there before.

This aroused his curiosity of course. He leaned down and cautiously explored with his spade, with the result that the visible stones collapsed further into the sand. Then he saw they had stood around an inner underground chamber, quite small, 'like a stone safe'.

We can picture him now – his spade still grasped in the strong, weathered hands typical of his calling – kneeling down, the better to peer into this cavity. All must have appeared dark at first, his eyes were probably dazzled by light reflecting off the sea. Then, in the darkness, he saw, gazing up at him with glistening, protuberant eyes of hypnotic quality, an array of small, motionless, pallid people in strange garb. They wore gowns with pleats, or armour. Crowns, helmets, mitres, tall caps decked their heads. All carried weapons or ritual objects – swords, daggers, shields, drinking cups, crooks like melting candles. One weird pygmy woman had arms folded in a witchlike way. One tiny moustachioed warrior was mounted on a miniature horse, its head down, as if petrified at the very moment of a battle charge.

From behind the astonished crofter came the remorseless heavy breathing of the sea . . .

Is it to be wondered at that his blood curdled, that he gripped – or dropped – his spade, and fled from that spine-chilling sight?

The miniature army

Fortunately for archaeology, he fled only as far as the arms of his wife. She had not been subjected to the strange influences of that day on the lonely dunes. She was able to calm him. And it soon occurred to her that the creatures her husband described might be something other than the dread Wee Folk, and might even be of some value. She persuaded him to go back to the stone cupboard in the dunes.

He did return, and this time the dreaded goblin gang turned out to be 78 exquisitely carved chessmen of walrus ivory. There were also fourteen draughts pieces and an ivory buckle.

We can buy replicas of them to-day – at a price – in the British Museum, where most of the pieces are on display, though eleven were acquired by the National Museum of Antiquities in Edinburgh.

They are believed to date from between 1135 and 1150 AD and constitute the finest early complete set of chessmen ever discovered. They were probably carved in Scandinavia. The fact that they show no signs of wear is puzzling. They must have been part of a travelling merchant's stock-in-hand.

Shall we ever find out how they got into a 'stone safe' in a sand-dune in the province of Uig?

It seems unlikely. But a story exists that, years before, a murder took place at that very spot. Here we leave archaeology, but it is a fascinating digression. A herdsman is said to have killed the survivor from a shipwreck, whom he found gasping on the shore, because he refused to give up to him the bundle he was clutching. Perhaps the survivor was a foreigner, and they could not communicate, so misunderstanding arose – or perhaps the herdsman was just a greedy, brutal killer. After the murder, the bundle, when shaken open, proved to contain the chessmen.

Their hypnotic, glaring eyes stared up at him, searching out his guilt. He jumped to the conclusion that they were the exotic idols of his victim, and he was so terrified of their powers that he went to a great deal of trouble to hide them in a secret place, underground.

Left. *One of the loneliest parts of Britain, the brooding coastline of the Isle of Lewis seems a most unlikely spot for the discovery of the Lewis chessmen.*

He was haunted by them, nevertheless, throughout his life. When about to be hanged for a subsequent murder, he blurted out a confession to the earlier one and mentioned the small, weird figures. The confession was noted, but the islanders decided to let the whole subject well alone.

As we have seen, the indestructible little ivory cohort, in spite of all efforts to suppress them, re-emerged in the fullness of time, when their re-discovery, unlike their incarceration, was not kept secret.

The truth of it all seems known now only to the chessmen.

The villa at Lullingstone

The Lullingstone 'treasure' again reveals a vision – no dream – of the past. Other fine country houses have been found up and down Roman Britain, but none as large as Lullingstone, in Kent, nor as rich in information to us. It represents the epitome of arts of living lost after the collapse of the Roman Empire.

Something differentiates it from all the rest of the many homes of consequence that graced Britain after 43 A.D. There is a certain dramatic strength about it. Its long connections with farming link it profoundly with the soil on which it flourished. Its religious aspect is uncommon. Its setting was particularly happy – on a gentle hillside, overlooking the sparkling waters of the River Darenth. Some of the finds are of a rare nature.

Land on the sunny slope had to be terraced in order to accommodate the house and its outbuildings, and later its temples. The villa, therefore, boasted – so to say – split-level foundations. When it fell into disuse, the earth gradually absorbed it; with soil-creep occurring downwards from the top of the bank. The designer, however, obviously appreciated the need to resist soil pressure on the structure and had incorporated strong retaining walls which were buried intact – some to a height of eight feet. This is a very uncommon circumstance, a bonus indeed in a Roman dig in this country. Romano-British research has benefited enormously from this one feature of Lullingstone alone, because prior to the excavation, the style

Right. *Undoubtedly the finest treasure from Lullingstone is this mosaic depicting Bellepheron slaying the Chimaera.*

of that period of Romano-British interior decoration was mainly a matter of conjecture.

There the walls stand; rendered with plaster over clay; some decorated with fragile fresco paintings of great beauty, some with pillared porticos, dados, painted wreaths and borders, corner decorations ... The handrail and skirting leading down to two cult rooms (pagan chapels), is a brilliant example of the adoption of an elegant form of decoration customary in Italy.

The site was discovered in the middle of the 18th century. A park fence was being built. Holes had to be driven to contain timber posts. Two were rammed in. Summer's head, no doubt as charmingly executed as the three other heads representing the other seasons, at the corner of the great mosaic showing Bellepheron slaying the Chimaera, is missing forever. The downdriven posts smashed straight into the mosaic floor of the reception room.

However, the discovery and location of the mosaic's tesserae were duly noted down by the antiquary John Thorpe. His notes were followed up by planned excavation – but not until nearly two centuries later. Englishmen take time.

Lullingstone was a home for many years before the Roman invasion. The original farmhouse and barns were built of timber and thatch. Intermittently, throughout its development, its owners reverted to agriculture.

The first farmers gradually became first more prosperous, then more Romanised. The first time a durable house of flint and mortar went up was between 80 and 90 A.D. The little circular temple on the lower terrace above and behind the house was probably built during the second century. It was a place of worship – traces of ritual fires have been found within – but of whom, or what, we cannot be sure. No doubt it was some pastoral deity, such as those shown in paintings in the house itself – nymphs crowned with leaves, wearing blue necklaces; one of them has water springing from her breasts. Such deities are in keeping with the peace which covers the site. The Darenth Valley is still a lovely, secluded corner of agricultural Kent; a place of sylvan allure.

A pagan burial

The big, square temple mausoleum on the upper terrace resembles in the main many of its kind which were attached to properties of consequence. An ambulatory surrounded this Romano-Celtic edifice, with its distinctive, domed roof covering the cult room. Inside it, in a subterranean chamber, were put the lead coffins and grave goods of two young people, a man and a woman in their early twenties. We do not know the cause of their death. Their pagan burial around 300 A.D. added a touch of sadness to the environment.

At some later date the tomb collapsed, and the young woman's body was disturbed by robbers. They threw back her bones, though, with some of the stolen lead. The young man's remains were not found by them, because a collapsed outer covering to the two tombs concealed his coffin from their view. His grave goods were all present on excavation. Of special rarity is his set of gaming pieces, of coloured glass on a square gaming board. It is the only complete set of such pieces to have come down to us from Roman Britain. The pair had been provided with all necessities for life hereafter – a flagon each, one of pottery, the other of bronze; four glass bottles with dolphin handles; two knives; two spoons; and two glass bowls. This careful provision for another world was made two centuries after the rites in the circular temple.

About 180 A.D. a person of Mediterranean origin, a rich and cultivated man, became the owner of Lullingstone. He brought to it much of the expansive warmth of the south. No longer a farm, the villa under his domination was considerably extended. Baths, kitchens, and cult rooms were added to it. Also, he brought with him two marble busts – portraits, it can be assumed, of his ancestors. The marble is Pentelic Greek marble, and the two heads are dignified – they date from the second century. Nothing like them is known elsewhere, and they have never been identified. They indicate the commanding type of the Mediterranean occupier's family and background, and their connection with the life of the villa was to become even closer in later years.

Right. *Pagan ritual and Christian worship were practised equally at Lullingstone in the 3rd century A.D. This marble bust, of an ancestor of one of the early owners of the villa, was worshipped as a cult figure, while at the same time, in another part of the villa, a form of Christian service was enacted – a reflection of the confused beliefs of this period.*

Splendour and decay

Their descendant stamped his personality on Lullingstone and he was to have a successor worthy of his mettle. Towards the end of the third century, a new owner, probably a Romano-Briton, restored the farming economy and made numerous alterations and additions to what was now a genuinely historic building. Not least of these was the adaptation of the Deep Room.

The Deep Room, so called because of the peculiarity of its dimensions, probably originated as a storehouse for grain. It lay now in the heart of the house, and a small platform which once jutted into it had long ago been removed. From the upper story, a flight of tiled stairs led into its depths.

The new owner covered in the back wall, sealing off the stairs, but for three of the bottom steps. These, left projecting, formed shelves. Here the old marble busts were arrayed, with votive pots in front of them. They had evolved into cult objects.

Later still, near the end of the following century, the Deep Room was again changed by being divided horizontally into two, by the insertion of a new floor. The chamber formed thus on the upper level was freshly and delicately decorated as a Christian chapel. Wall paintings included a large sacred monogram, the Chi Rho, representing the first two Greek letters of Christ's name. The chamber was approached by a vestibule and an ante-room, the latter also adorned with a painted representation of the Chi Rho. But at ground level, in the lower half of the Deep Room, the marble busts remained on their curious 'shelves' with their votive pots in position. Thus, above and below, pagan and Christian worship proceeded simultaneously. This is a very odd occurrence.

Yet another century passed. The sowing and harvesting of crops, the lowing of cattle watering in the Darenth, the peaceful aura of fat Kent sheep ceased to sweeten Lullingstone. Farming was discontinued. With its cessation, other activity too seemed to ebb away from house and grounds. Signs of occupation dwindled, but it

Right. *Guarded by ditches and ramparts, the huge mass of Maiden Castle must have seemed an impregnable fortress to its defenders. But the better-armed Romans took the fort and turned it into a mass grave.*

Above. *Sadness is the overlying mood of Maiden Castle now. These two skeletons, butchered by the Romans, were buried together in a last fond gesture by the survivors of the massacre.*

may be that, for a while, worship continued in the Christian rooms.

Then, abruptly, as at Fishbourne, everything came to a full-stop after a devastating conflagration. Again, we do not know what caused it. The villa blazed into a charred ruin and slowly sank away out of sight and memory.

However, the final conclusion cannot be a despairing one. At Lullingstone, not only was life lived – piety alternating with pleasure – but is seen again to have been so lived, nearly two thousand years later.

Maiden Castle

The drama of Maiden Castle belongs to a much more primitive era. To turn to it after wandering through the Roman palace and villa is like turning an early metal mirror to its unburnished side. We leave harbour and valley, commerce and colour. We forget indulgence in refined surroundings. We retreat to an Iron Age fortress on high ground in a wild Dorset, where life is still regulated by the ways, thoughts and beliefs of nomadic tribes – for at its beginning Maiden Castle was a camp for cattle-gatherers.

Later it became one vast burial mound, over 5 feet high, and of the astonishing length of nearly 2,000 feet. At the eastern end of this neolithic long barrow, a neolithic skeleton was found. Its limbs were hacked off, and the brain had been brutally, but thoroughly scraped out of the skull. It is conceivable there is a link here with pagan cannabalism in some form. The skeleton can be seen in Dorchester Museum. It typifies the fate of Maiden Castle, which was to become a cemetery. It invokes the castle's climate of sacrifice, isolation, defiance and terror.

In its cattle-herding days, when the sun shone and larks climbed from the aromatic turf, Maiden Castle must have been a peaceful place. There were certainly battles, for the hilltop was prepared for them with ditches and ramparts, but they would have been sporadic skirmishes of a tribal nature. Centuries passed; settlers came and went. About 250 B.C. about 16 acres on the height to the east were permanently inhabited – the remains of huts and traces of settled cooking have been found, including a bun of bread. A rampart was round this settlement, 12 feet high, faced with timber, and this in its turn was surrounded by a deep, wide ditch. Soon all the 45 acres of the plateau were settled and fortified in a similar manner, and the fortifications steadily continued to be strengthened with ever more elaborate ramparts and barbicans.

About 150 years later, the defences became so strong and incorporated so many new features that it appears as if some new influence had been exerted. According to Sir Mortimer Wheeler, the new ideas may have been introduced by refugee Gauls, a handful of the Veneti from Brittany, who escaped and made their way to southern England after their decisive defeat by Julius Caesar at Quiberon Bay. Only in Brittany have similar deposits of sling-stones been found in association with comparable defences.

Slings against the Legions

The Veneti literally knew all about 'the slings and arrows of outrageous fortune'. They had confidence in the effectiveness of sling-stones hurled across ramparts and ditches, from their long-successful defence against Caesar in their cliff-castles on rocky, lonely promontories in Brittany. By its position, and already formidable fortifications, Maiden Castle could have seemed an ideal place for such desperate veterans to utilise.

However, when the day came that Maiden Castle was rushed by the legions of Vespasian, the Romans were armed with the catapult, or lesser scorpion – the powerful new weapon which could send iron bolts humming lethally across more than thirty yards. Even the settler's now huge and intricate system of encircling defences could not repel the attack.

The ditches were stormed, the ramparts scaled, even against the dogged hail of sling-stones. The vanquished were savagely massacred. The Roman soldiers seem to have taken a most violent revenge for the obstinate opposition they had to overcome. Ruthless slaughter ensued; the evidence of it in moving contrast to that of the luxury enjoyed by romanised Britons in other *oppida* which had already succumbed to Vespasian.

Where, in all this, is to be found 'buried treasure'?

There is only the proof of haunting solidarity in the Britons' attempts to bury their dead after the siege. For, those who had survived the holocaust returned when darkness descended, to pay what homage they could to the slain.

38 bodies of women as well as of men have been recovered – all bearing terrible wounds. They had all received some gesture of respect, even of tender treatment. There can have been little time for the survivors to do more than search them out, then attempt at least to deposit them decently, if not to lay them out and bury them.

Those who performed these last services must have been shaking with grief, horror and exhaustion. Yet good joints of lamb were judiciously selected from the food-stocks, and placed in the hands of the dead, to sustain them in the worlds beyond the battlefields. Personal trinkets of some value, such as iron toe-rings, amulets, armlets and finger-rings were left with the dead. One male skeleton seems to bear witness to a touch of love. He was buried in a double grave. Beside him were placed his battle-axe and his knife. Balanced with care on his breast was a small bronze ear-pick.

Maiden Castle is not only the first British war cemetery, it is one of the finest Iron Age forts in Europe. In spite of the absence of jewels and gold, many of the discoveries made there are of incalculable value for the light they throw on the centuries preceding, and up to the Roman conquest.

Today, as we contemplate the calm, green, empty slopes of Maiden Castle, still so nobly protected by its great ramparts, certain minor items alone, incontrovertibly attesting to human feeling and courage in a lost cause, seem 'buried treasure' enough.

LOST PIRATE HOARDS

Windsor Chorlton

Above. *Captain William Kidd pleads his case before the House of Commons. It was in vain – political expediency demanded that he die.*

The popular image of treasure and treasure hunting – of intrepid explorers, faded parchment maps and a tropical island marked with a cross – is largely false. But the fascination of the unknown and the lure of untold wealth still compel people to believe in such fabulous treasures as the lost city of Eldorado, or in the equally fantastic King Solomon's Mines.

In fact these and other legendary hoards appear to have some basis in fact; but they have become so blurred by time and over-active imaginations that it is now impossible to separate fact from fiction. And one thing which distinguishes today's treasure hunters from the fictional characters of one's adolescent reading, is that the serious treasure hunter deals in facts.

But the romantic image of treasure is a compelling one, and while there are still mysteries to be solved and the possibility of vast riches looms large in the imagination, there will always be an individual prepared to sacrifice everything in his quest. For such a treasure hunter the choice of potential hoards is vast; but some treasures exert a stronger fascination than the rest – among them the legendary hoards of the Caribbean pirates.

A gentleman privateer

On 23 May 1701, a pirate named William Kidd sat in his cell in Newgate prison writing a last desperate appeal to the Speaker of the House of Commons. He asked that he be allowed to return, under escort, to the West Indies, where he claimed to have 'lodged goods and Tresure to the Value of one hundred thousand pounds, which I desiere the Government may have the benefit of ...' But despite the promise of treasure, the appeal was ignored and Kidd was hanged a few hours later.

Researchers into Kidd's dramatic life are sceptical of his claims; they argue that the pirate was simply, and understandably, trying to save his neck. The records show, they point out, that at the time of Kidd's arrest, a vast hoard of his treasure was discovered in Long Island – treasure which amounted to 200 bars of gold, bags of precious stones; as well as bales of exotic cloths and thousands of silver coins. At first glance it does seem unlikely that Kidd had concealed more than one hoard; but despite the sceptics' claims, the search for Kidd's treasure goes on – a fact which can be explained by the peculiar circumstances of his life.

Kidd was probably born in Scotland about 1645. The first clear reference to him dates from 1689 and describes him as a 'Gentleman'. Obviously Kidd's early life was both respectable and profitable: by astute merchant trading with the Indies, and a successful marriage to a wealthy widow he became a pillar of New York society. But hidden beneath the facade of the merchant was an adventurer; for Kidd had led several raiding expeditions against the French, as a privateer working for the British.

The line separating privateers and pirates was a thin one. Ostensibly, privateers worked for their governments to secure trade and colonial rights from enemy states. They operated on privately owned vessels and carried Letters of Marque authorizing them to capture enemy shipping. This unofficial navy was encouraged to bring their prizes to a colonial port, where the booty was divided between the privateers and the government officials. Few privateers, however, distinguished between ships of their own and other countries and, protected by their Letters of Marque, they plundered anything they felt strong enough to attack.

But until 1695, William Kidd appeared to operate strictly within the law. His standing in the community rose and he made many influential friends – among them a man called Robert Livingstone. It was Livingstone who was to initiate the ill-fated scheme which would lead to a public scandal in England and the death of Kidd on the gallows.

Kidd turns pirate

Livingstone's scheme, to which he devoted all his immense energy, was that Kidd should lead a privateering expedition against the notorious pirates Blackbeard, Teach, Bradish and others. Such an ambitious plan required money, and Livingstone sailed for London to persuade the newly elected Governor of New York, the Earl of Bellamont, to sponsor his plan. He was successful; not only was the Earl of Bellamont enthusiastic, but he also persuaded the First Lord of the Admiralty, the Chancellor and Lord Keeper of the Great Seal, the Secretary of State, and the Master General of the Ordnance to finance the expedition to the tune of £6,000. Kidd received his commission, and with the rather wishful order 'to refrain from molesting our friends and allies', he sailed from Plymouth in the *Adventure Galley*.

But things went wrong. After picking up a motley crew of ruffians in New York, Kidd sailed for the Indian Ocean where, for a whole year, he failed to capture a prize. The crew, who had signed on a 'no prize, no pay' agreement, became increasingly mutinous, and the capture of a small Moorish vessel did not satisfy them.

Even this small capture created problems. The Portuguese, on hearing of it, ordered a man-of-war to intercept the privateer. Kidd was forced to fight a long battle with the more heavily-armed ship, and though he managed to break away, the *Adventure Galley* was badly damaged and the crew more dissatisfied than ever.

Although Kidd must have been conscious of the threat from his crew, he continued to obey

Decamps

Imp.^e par Chardon.

Pirates

his command to avoid friendly shipping. After capturing another Moorish ship which sailed under French orders, he refused to attack a Dutch ship – the result was a near-mutiny, which Kidd avoided by the drastic measure of killing his gunner with a bucket.

It was after this incident that Kidd began his career of piracy, for after capturing an Armenian ship, the *Quedah Merchant,* and sharing the loot amongst his rebellious crew, he sailed for Madagascar – one of the favourite pirate bases. If he had fulfilled his commission, Kidd would have attempted to seize some of the pirates he met on the island. Instead he was welcomed as an old friend, and after resting his crew he transferred to the *Quedah Merchant* and set sail for New York.

By now Kidd knew he was a hunted man. The *Quedah Merchant* had been commanded by an Englishman and news of its capture incensed the Admiralty. They immediately declared him a pirate and though, later, a general amnesty was declared on buccaneers, Kidd was specifically exempted. He was not unduly worried; Bellamont and Robert Livingstone would exert

Left. *Pirates attack a merchant ship. Such an occurrence was accepted as part of the risks of trade in the 17th century.*

Rouargue Jne

2ᵉ V P 7

their influence on his behalf, and besides, the treasure he carried would buy his freedom.

But the golden age of piracy was drawing to a close. Buccaneers who harried the Spaniards had once been tolerated, even encouraged; but the war was long over and pirates were now considered a menace on the seas and an embarrassment at home. When Kidd arrived in New York he was arrested by his former mentor, Lord Bellamont.

Kidd claimed that he gave the Governor some of his pirate booty, but clearly Bellamont felt that Kidd had concealed most of his loot, and under increasing pressure from England, he shipped his prisoner to London to face trial.

The trial was a public sensation, and a great deal of political capital was made out of it. To the Whigs in power and the Navy, which had largely sponsored his expedition, Kidd was a source of acute embarrassment. The pirate pleaded in vain that the ships he had taken carried French passes and were, therefore, a legitimate prize. After a year in prison – a year during which the First Lord of the Admiralty and the Chancellor and Lord of the Great Seal were impeached for their part in the expedition – Kidd was executed.

Kidd's mysterious island

Did Kidd bury a vast hoard of treasure? Apart from the claims he made in his death-cell appeal there are several other facts to be considered. Firstly, Kidd was no fool. Although he expected the protection of his former employers, he must have been acutely suspicious of them. It would only have been logical if Kidd had concealed some of his booty before returning to America. As for the rejection of his promise to lead his captors to his hoard, the government could hardly have accepted a financial deal during such a politically delicate time.

But nobody takes a reputed treasure hoard seriously unless there is some clue to its location – and where treasure is concerned that usually means a map, preferably of old parchment. Such a map exists; in fact there are three of them, and all depict the same island.

The maps were all obtained from genuine old sea-chests which bore Kidds name. In the best romantic tradition they depict an island situated somewhere in the China Sea; and while they do not contradict each other, each chart carries information which is not included in the others.

The most complete chart, discovered in 1934, gives not only the position of the treasure island in latitude and longitude, but reputedly marks the location of the treasure.

Why then, if these supposedly genuine charts have been found, has William Kidd's treasure not been recovered? There are three main reasons for this failure. Firstly, although the most complete chart shows the latitude and longitude of the island, these bearings were calculated before Greenwich became the standardised point from which latitude was calculated. Although attempts have been made to translate the bearings given on the chart to the present-day standard, the results have been inconclusive and have not revealed the island shown on Kidd's original charts.

Secondly, even if the island had been found, the location of the treasure, as depicted on the charts, is vague, and the coded directions obscure. It is unlikely that even the most skilled cypher expert could use the instructions given on the charts to pin-point the treasure.

Finally, Kidd's privateering expedition of 1696-1699 was, as far as is known, confined to the Atlantic and Indian Oceans: there is no record of him visiting the China Sea – where his island is situated – between these dates.

An unsolved mystery

These inconsistencies raise fresh speculation. Did Kidd, in fact, bury a treasure on an island nearer his home coast of America – perhaps in the Caribbean – and mark its location in the China Sea simply to confuse those who might steal or chance upon his charts? Advocates of this theory point out that not only does it explain the failure of treasure hunters to identify Kidd's island in the China Sea, but also that Kidd was unlikely to have hidden a treasure hoard so far from home.

There are many who still believe that Kidd's charts were accurate and that eventually his island will be found. This group claims that the treasure indicated on the map never belonged to Kidd, and that the privateer had found the charts on one of his earlier privateering missions. They assert that Kidd undertook his last

Right. *Henry Morgan – probably the most successful pirate of all time. From a humble beginning as a plantation worker, he was to be created Lieutenant Governor of Jamaica.*

IUAN MORGAN

The Towne of Puerto del Principe taken & sackt

But to many people the charts are simply a fraud – an elaborate practical joke at the expense of the more gullible treasure hunter. They argue, with some justification, that to find one treasure chart is just possible, but that to find three – all recovered from sea-chests belonging to Kidd – is stretching credibility too far.

The arguments go on. Kidd's legendary treasure is now so much a part of the folk-lore on both sides of the Atlantic, that even if the available evidence were to be totally discredited, the stories would persist. People like a mystery – and few things are as mysterious as the story of Captain William Kidd and his elusive treasure.

Henry Morgan – buccaneer

Not all pirates ended on the gallows: one of the most successful of them all, Henry Morgan, died peacefully in his bed at Port Royal, Jamaica. Looking back on his career as he lay dying, Morgan must have felt few regrets; for packed into the space of 53 years, this buccaneer-turned-politician had lived the kind of extravagantly adventurous life found only in the pages of the most lurid fiction.

After his death, the legends about Morgan grew. In England he had always been a popular figure and soon he came to personify the swashbuckling hero who, almost 300 years later, would become the model for extravagant Hollywood pirate epics. It was only natural that stories about a great treasure which Morgan had hidden would become common; but though most of them were patently untrue, one at least deserves careful examination.

Morgan was born in South Wales in 1635. Little is known about his early life, but it is probable that he either joined or was press-ganged onto a ship sailing for the West Indies. Reports that he was transported to the colonies for some youthful felony may be true because, bearing in mind his subsequent stormy career, it seems unlikely that the peace of a quiet Welsh town would have satisfied him for long.

In Barbados, Morgan joined up with Colonel Robert Venable's army and took part in the capture of Jamaica and the assault on St Jago in

Left. *Morgan's success as a buccaneer was based on his genius as a military strategist. However, although he succeeded in taking the town of Puerto del Principe in one of his first raids as leader of the Port Royal privateers, booty was scarce and his troops dissatisfied.*
Above. *A Spanish ship fights off a pirate craft.*

commission only in order to locate and recover the treasure shown on the charts. Again, this is a feasible theory as it explains why Kidd – who at the time of his commission was a successful merchant – should have undertaken such a hazardous mission. It also explains why Kidd did not elaborate on the location of the treasure in his death-cell appeal – he did not know the precise location any more than the present owners of the charts.

Overleaf. *A French map of the Panama Isthmus. None of the inhabitants of Panama City believed it was possible to be attacked from the Caribbean – Morgan was to prove them wrong.*

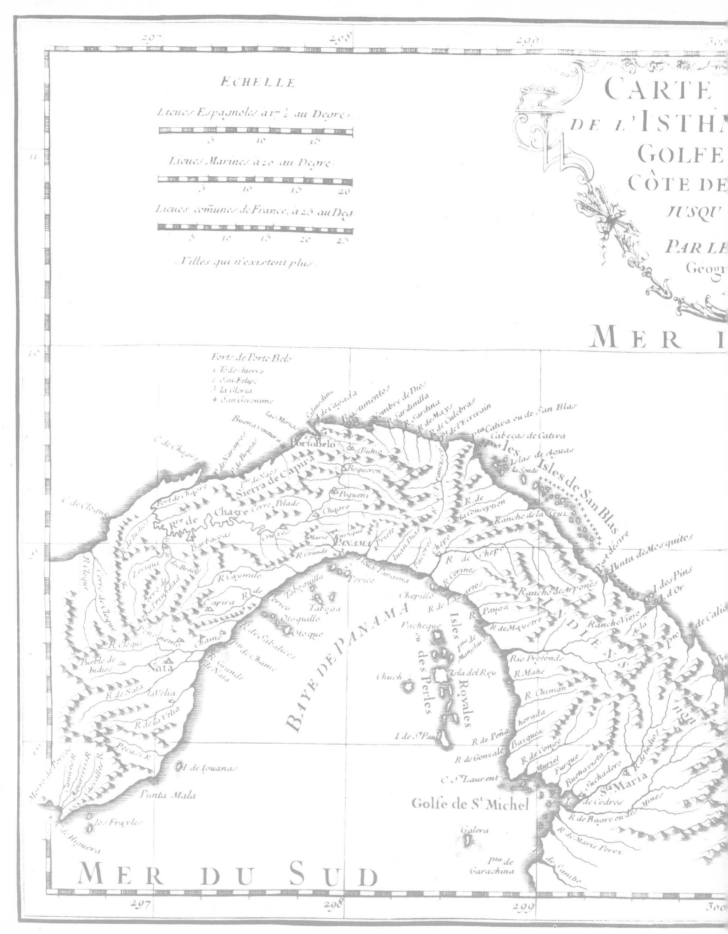

ECHELLE

Lieues Espagnoles a 17 ½ au Degré
5   10   15

Lieues Marines à 20 au Degré
5   10   15   20

Lieues comunes de France, à 25 au Deg.
5   10   15   20   25

Villes qui n'existent plus.

CARTE
DE L'ISTHM
GOLFE
à
CÔTE DE
JUSQU
PAR LE
Geogr

MER I

Forts de Porto Belo.
1 To do Fuerro
2 San Felive
3 La Gloria
4 San Geronime

Buenaventura   las Marias   Calmedma   de Casada   Instrumentos   Nombre de Dios   Sardinilla
C. de Chagre   Pte Naranies   R. de Brenas   R. Sardina
PortoBelo   el Buho   R. de Mays   R. de Culebras   Pt del Escrivain   Pta Cativa ou de San Blas
C. de Cloque   Pte de Nace   Boqueron   Cabecas de Cativa
Sierra de Capura   Pequeni   Isles de San Blas
Fort de chagre   Cerro Pelade   R. de   Islas de Aguas
Rte de Chagre   Chagre   la Sonde
Barbacoa   Cruzes   Marie Enrique   Conception   Ranche de la Cruz
R. de Bono   R. Grande   PANAMA   Prete   Juan Dias   Facore   R. de   Port Escuré
R. Chagre   Levini   R. Caymilo   Perice   Islas Panama   Chepo   R. de Chepo   Junta de Mosquites
Cerro de Cloque   la Trinidad   R. de Perice   Tabequilla   R. Corines   Rancho de Arzones   I des Pins
Capira   Tabega   Chepillo   R. de Lavartes   Payva   d Or
R. Cloque   Penonomo   Otoquillo   Pacheque   R. de Mavre   Ranche Viejo   de Calib
Pueblo de Indios   Chame   Otoque   Manzlar   Rio Profonde   Acla
Nata   Pte de Chame   Chuch   Isla del Rey   R. Mahé
R. de Nata   R. Grande   BAYE DE PANAMA   Isles Royales   R. Ouman
la Velia   de Nata   Isles   ou des Perles   horada   St Maria
R. de la Velia   des Perles   Buenavista   Ouchadero
Pecas R.   I de St Paul   R. de Peña   Barquez   Muriel   Furque   de Cedros
O I de Louana.   R. de Gonzale   R. de Conge   R. de Baore ou des Mines
Punta Mala   C. St Laurent   R. de Marie Perez
Jos Frayles   Golfe de St Michel   R. de Cambo
P. de Higuera   Galera

MER DU SUD

Pta de Garachina

112

Hispaniola. His courage and qualities of leadership were apparent, for 12 years later, at the age of 31, when he had left the army, Morgan was appointed second-in-command to Captain Edward Mansveldt, leader of the Port Royal privateers.

Morgan's early career as a privateeer was not particularly successful. An attempt to capture the city of Porto Bello in 1665 was foiled by a leak in intelligence, which prompted the President of Panama to strongly garrison the city. However, Morgan's stature as a leader grew, and on Mansveldt's death he was given command of the privateering fleet.

But many Dutch and French privateers refused to accept his authority because England was at war with their countries. Deprived of the support of a large part of his force, Morgan was confined to capturing local Spanish shipping. Then, in 1667, England made peace with Holland and France – Morgan was able to plan his first big mission.

By this time, news of the privateer's exploits had spread throughout the Caribbean and, always ready to strengthen Britain's position in the West Indies, the Governor of Jamaica, Sir Thomas Modyford, gave Morgan the rank of Colonel and endorsed his privateering activities. With this official sanction, Morgan attacked Puerto Principé in Cuba; but although the assault was a military success, little booty was gained.

On his return to Port Royal, Morgan realized that before he could completely win the confidence of his men, he had to offer them more than just bloody battles. And so, in a brilliantly conceived and executed assault on Porto Bello, Morgan's privateers captured more than 250,000 pieces of eight as well as a hoard of other valuable merchandise. The former plantation-worker now had the total trust of his men and he could begin planning his most ambitious enterprise; a mission which had defeated even the legendary Sir Francis Drake – an attack on Panama.

Assault on Panama

Panama was situated on the Pacific coast of the isthmus and its inhabitants must have felt im-

Left. *Although they outnumbered Morgan's force, the garrison at Panama fell an easy prey to the untrained but brilliantly led buccaneers.*

mune to an attack from the Caribbean. But to a brilliant strategist like Morgan, the daunting journey across the isthmus was more than compensated for by the certainty that the Spanish garrison would almost certainly be surprised by his army.

Morgan laid his plans well. He ordered part of his force to occupy the fort of San Lorenzo, at the mouth of the Chagres River, while the rest of his men built boats to take them part of the way to Panama. With the fleet at San Lorenzo guarding his rear, Morgan, with over 1,000 men, began the long haul up the Chagres.

Two days later they were within 24 miles of their goal; but shoals and sunken logs prevented further progress up-river and they were forced to make a hazardous and difficult journey overland. Morale on the journey sank so low that many of the privateers begged to return to the ships; and by the end of the journey their food was exhausted and they were forced to boil and eat their leather bags.

But Morgan's forced march was rewarded: although the Spaniards knew of the approaching army, they were not prepared for it and the defenders were soon routed. On the tenth day after leaving the Chagres River the privateers took Panama.

It is at this point that the mystery of the Panama treasure develops. The city was the richest in the New World – a vast warehouse for the wealth extracted from the conquered kingdom of the Incas. Silver, mined at Potosi, and gold were carried to Panama by mule train to await shipment to Spain. The city itself testified to its wealth, for despite its isolation in this far-flung corner of the Spanish Empire, it boasted 2,000 houses owned by merchants, two richly ornamented churches and eight monasteries. And yet, despite the affluence of the city, Morgan and his men reported a pitifully small prize.

One reason for this failure to capture the amount of booty expected has been ascribed to the great fire which swept through Panama shortly after the privateers entered it. Although Morgan was blamed for the blaze, which destroyed most of the city, the privateer angrily explained later that he was unlikely to destroy

Left. *Panama burns. Later, Morgan vehemently denied that he had been responsible for destroying the greater part of the city.*

the city he had risked his life to loot. It is more probable that the Governor of Panama ordered the fire when he knew the city was lost.

Another explanation for the disappointing amount of loot which Morgan carried back to Jamaica, was the failure of the privateers to prevent treasure ships leaving the port. It is almost certain that such ships did manage to avoid attack, but whether the citizens of Panama had enough time to load their possessions on them is doubtful.

Other writers, sceptical of the stories that Morgan appropriated most of the booty for himself, point out that if the commander was satisfied with the haul, he certainly did not show it. In fact, Morgan conducted the most brutal tortures to extract the whereabouts of treasures from the citizens. Neither sex was exempt from his cruel interrogation and this episode alone should dispel the romantic aura which has grown up round the man.

The triumphant return

Morgan remained in Panama for a month while he sent out parties to search for valuables, tortured those citizens who he felt were concealing their possessions from him, and extracted ransoms from the relatives of those he held captive. By the end of this time he had collected some 750,000 pieces of eight, which were carried to his waiting ships by mule-train.

Then, satisfied that he had taken all the loot he was likely to find, and worried about the safety of his fleet, Morgan led his men back to the river. When the exhausted army reached their ships, the booty they had captured was divided amongst them. The shares were pitifully small considering the hardships the privateers had endured – a mere £10 per man – and, according to the Dutch buccaneer, Esquemeling, the pirates knew they had been cheated but dared not protest.

The allegations that Morgan cheated his men of their spoils is given added substance by the fact that, as soon as the plunder had been shared out, he left suddenly for Jamaica, leaving his fleet leaderless and without provisions. Furthermore, Morgan ordered the guns of San Lorenzo fort to be transferred to his own ship – a move which confirmed the suspicions of his men that he was carrying home a fabulously rich cargo. Whether or not Morgan stopped off at some deserted Caribbean island to bury a

percentage of his treasure is not known; but, as the privateer knew that his government would demand a share of the spoils, it seems a probable action.

Perhaps the British Government thought so too, because in 1672 the hero of Panama was sent home in the frigate *Welcome* to stand trial for piracy. But the forces of justice had not anticipated the popular appeal of Morgan. The man who had treated the citizens of Panama so barbarically was treated like a hero in England and, far from ending up on the gallows like Kidd, Morgan was eventually returned to Jamaica in the post of Lieutenant Governor.

So Morgan found respectability at last; and if his former colleagues expected him to encourage their privateering activities, they were sadly wrong. Times were changing, and Morgan did his utmost to convert Port Royal from a privateering base to a prosperous commercial centre. Disillusioned by their former leader, and conscious of the new threats to their piratical activities, a large number of buccaneers shifted their centre of operations to the isle of Tortuga.

Morgan grew old and wealthy on his vast Jamaican estates. In 1682 he retired from his post and spent most of the last years of his life drinking in the taverns of Port Royal. He died, aged 53, a pot-bellied alcoholic and was buried in the cemetry at Port Royal – a part of the history of the West Indies died with him.

Lost treasures of Port Royal

Morgan, as far as is known, left no clues to the whereabouts of any treasure, and though many of his associates talked about the vast wealth he had concealed in the Caribbean, they revealed no concrete evidence. Not that proof of Morgan's treasure hoard was needed, for during the 300 years since his death, many treasure hunters have searched for his elusive hoard. Occasionally, newspapers have reported that finds of gold coins in the Caribbean were buried by Morgan; but these reports owe more to journalistic licence than to hard facts. The truth is now so shrouded in the myths that grew up round the man that any new information about his reputed treasure must be viewed sceptically.

But there is a very strong link between Henry Morgan and a buried treasure. On a cloudless morning in June 1692, four years after the privateer's death, a violent earthquake destroyed Port Royal and buried part of it under the sea.

To the more law-abiding citizens of the town, the earthquake signified God's punishment of a place which, to them, was a sink of iniquity and wicked licentiousness. If Divine judgement was the cause of the disaster, it was extremely harsh: over 2,000 citizens perished, and half the town was lost – including the cemetery where Morgan was buried.

Years went by and many amateur salvors recovered objects from the sunken city. But no organised salvage attempt was made until 1965, when Robert Marx, one of the pioneer underwater treasure hunters and archeologists, was commissioned by the Government of Jamaica to excavate the site. In the first year of his work

Above. *Morgan interrogates a prisoner. After the capture of Panama it was widely alleged that he had tortured citizens in an effort to locate treasure. The allegations were probably true and should dispel the romantic aura which has grown up around the man.*

Marx made some amazing finds – including two sunken ships and a treasure chest; as well as a priceless collection of artefacts. Piecing together the evidence from his finds, Marx was able to reconstruct a vivid picture of 17th century life in the privateer port.

Did the chest which Marx discovered belong to Morgan? It is possible, as it bore the crest of

119

Above. *Robert Marx – marine archaeologist for the Jamaican government. Has he solved the mystery of Morgan's lost pirate hoard?*

the Spanish king and could well have been part of the plunder from Panama. The coins found inside the chest were mainly from the mines at Lima and Potosi and were all freshly minted. The inference is that they were never circulated and had, in fact, been buried almost immediately after they were captured.

Whether or not the coins belonged to Morgan is a matter of conjecture. The idea that part of the hoard which the buccaneers took from Panama has been found is an attractive one;

and makes a fitting end to the history of a pirate who ranks with Drake as one of the great naval commanders. But a large number of treasure hunters remain unconvinced and, for as long as the legend of Morgan's treasure persists, they will continue to search for it on the islands of the Caribbean.